CHURCHES OF BRISTOL

Maurice Fells

MAURICE FELLS

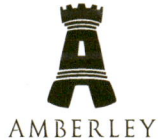

This edition first published 2025

Amberley Publishing
The Hill, Stroud
Gloucestershire GL5 4EP

www.amberley-books.com

Copyright © Maurice Fells, 2025

The right of Maurice Fells to be identified as the Author
of this work has been asserted in accordance with the
Copyrights, Designs and Patents Act 1988.

All rights reserved. No part of this book may be reprinted
or reproduced or utilised in any form or by any electronic,
mechanical or other means, now known or hereafter invented, including
photocopying and recording, or in any information
storage or retrieval system, without the permission in writing
from the Publishers.

British Library Cataloguing in Publication Data.
A catalogue record for this book is available from the British Library.

ISBN 978 1 3981 2231 4 (print)
ISBN 978 1 3981 2232 1 (ebook)

Typesetting by SJmagic DESIGN SERVICES, India.
Printed in Great Britain.

Appointed GPSR EU Representative:
Easy Access System Europe Oü, 16879218
Address: Mustamäe tee 50, 10621, Tallinn, Estonia
Contact Details: gpsr.requests@easproject.com, +358 40 500 3575

Contents

Map 4
Key 6
Introduction 7

1. Church of St James Priory, The Horsefair 9
2. The New Room or Wesley's Chapel, The Horsefair 11
3. St Peter's Church, Castle Park 14
4. St Mary Le Port, Castle Park 16
5. St John the Baptist, Broad Street 17
6. Temple Church, Temple Way 20
7. Christ Church with St Ewen, Broad Street 21
8. Hope Chapel, Hotwells 24
9. Holy Trinity Church, Hotwells Road 26
10. All Saints' Church, Corn Street 28
11. All Saints' Church, Clifton 29
12. Emmanuel Church, Clifton 32
13. Christ Church, Clifton 34
14. St Nicholas' Church, Baldwin Street 36
15. The Cathedral Church of St Peter and St Paul, Clifton 38
16. St Paul's Church, Southville 41
17. St Mary on the Quay, Colston Avenue 43
18. St Mark's Chapel (The Lord Mayor's Chapel), College Green 45
19. The Church of St George, Brandon Hill 49
20. St Peter's Church, Bishopsworth 51
21. St Michael the Archangel on the Mount Without, St Michael's Hill 52
22. St Stephen's Church, St Stephen's Avenue 54
23. Holy Trinity Church, Westbury-on-Trym 57
24. Bristol Cathedral, College Green 60
25. St Mary Redcliffe Church, Redcliffe 67
26. St Werburgh's Church, St Werburgh's 73
27. St Paul's Church, St Paul's 75
28. St Mary Magdalene, Stoke Bishop 77
29. Holy Trinity Church, Old Market 80
30. St Thomas the Martyr, Redcliffe 81
31. St Mary's Church, Shirehampton 83
32. Church of St Mary the Virgin, Henbury 84
33. St Alban's Church, Westbury Park 87
34. Redland Church, Redland 88
35. The Chapel of the Three Kings of Cologne, Colston Street 90

Bibliography 94
Acknowledgements 95
About the Author 96

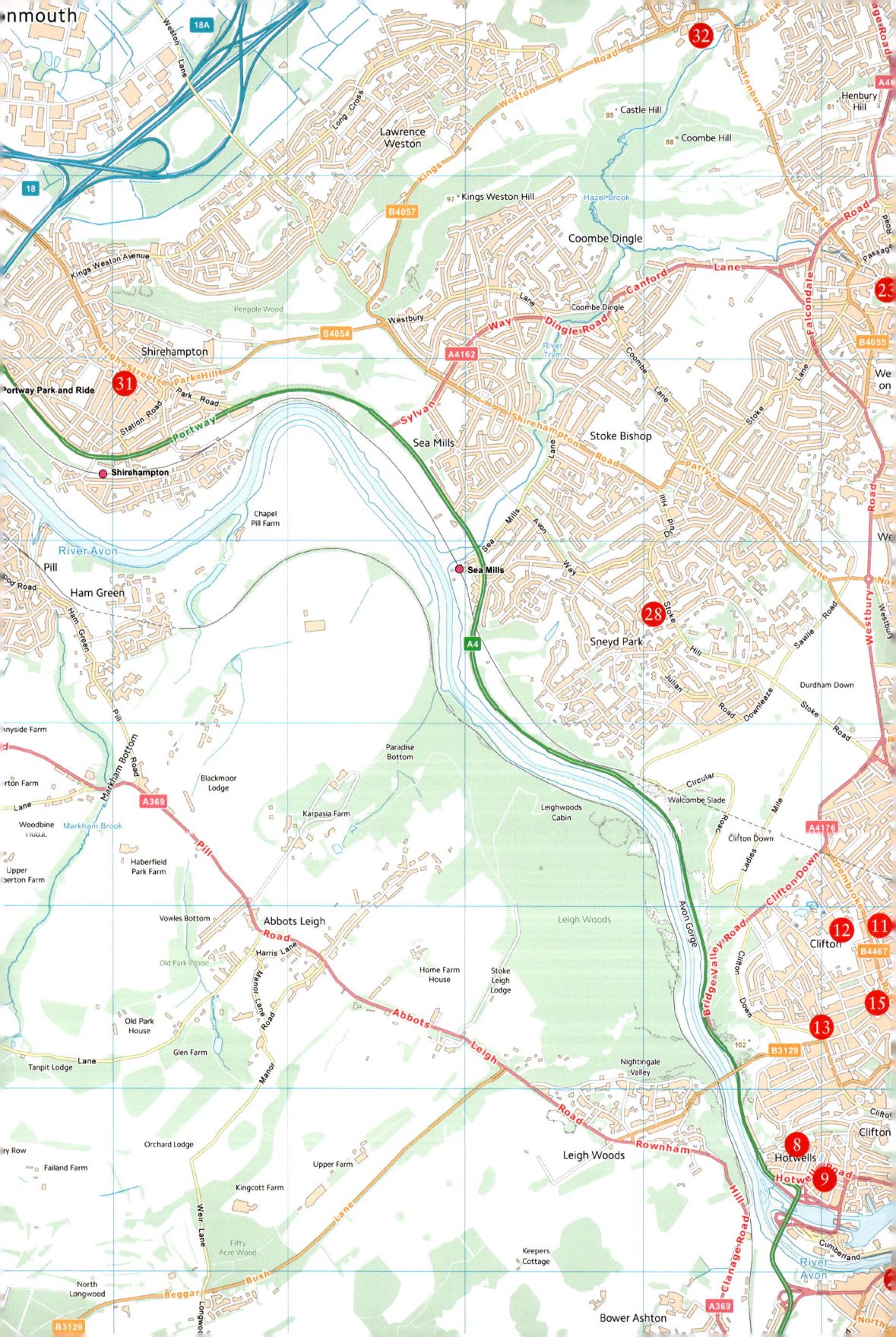

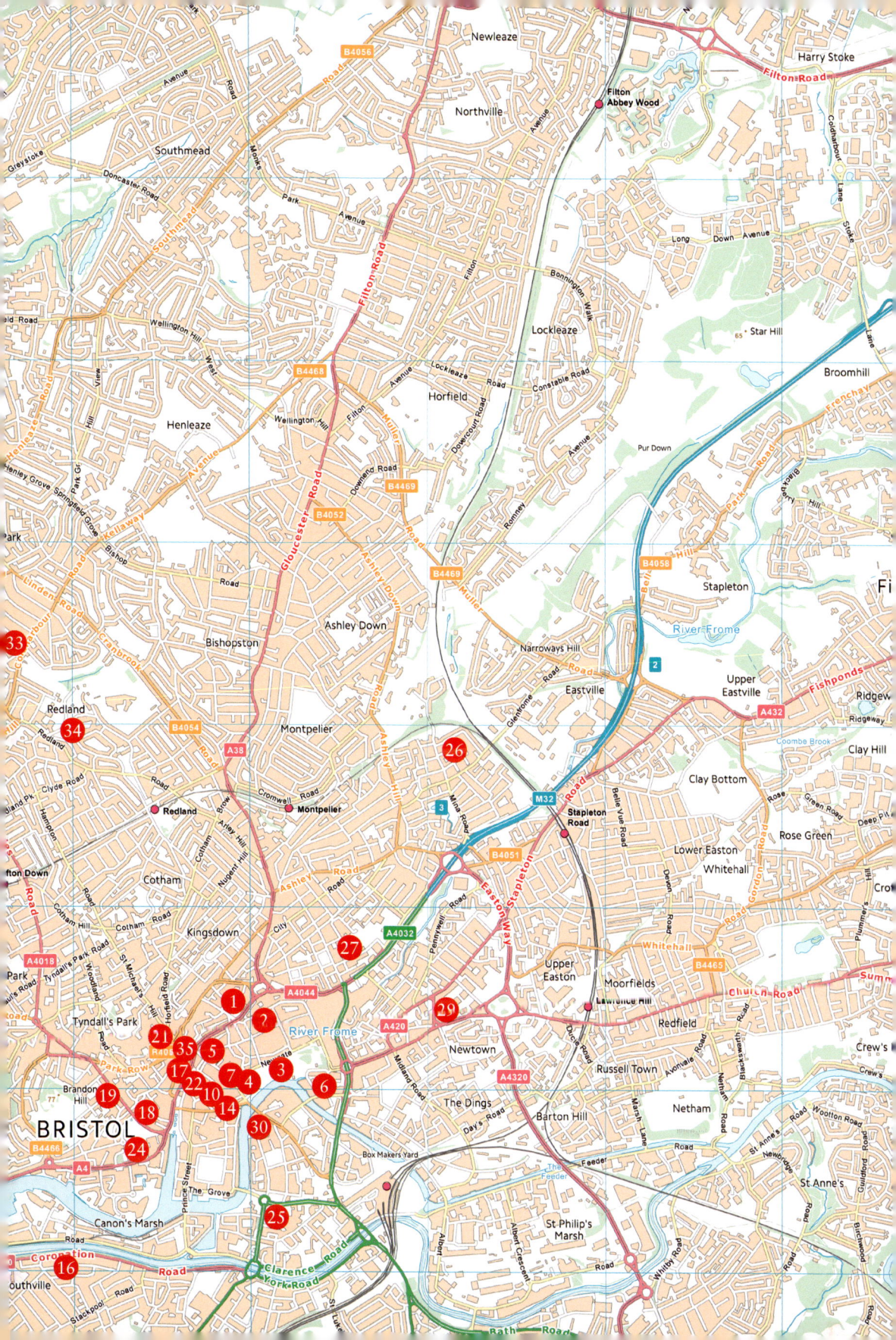

Key

1. Church of St James Priory, The Horsefair
2. The New Room or Wesley's Chapel, The Horsefair
3. St Peter's Church, Castle Park
4. St Mary Le Port, Castle Park
5. St John the Baptist, Broad Street
6. Temple Church, Temple Way
7. Christ Church with St Ewen, Broad Street
8. Hope Chapel, Hotwells
9. Holy Trinity Church, Hotwells Road
10. All Saints' Church, Corn Street
11. All Saints' Church, Clifton
12. Emmanuel Church, Clifton
13. Christ Church, Clifton
14. St Nicholas' Church, Baldwin Street
15. The Cathedral Church of St Peter and St Paul, Clifton
16. St Paul's Church, Southville
17. St Mary on the Quay, Colston Avenue
18. St Mark's Chapel (The Lord Mayor's Chapel), College Green
19. The Church of St George, Brandon Hill
20. St Peter's Church, Bishopsworth
21. St Michael the Archangel on the Mount Without, St Michael's Hill
22. St Stephen's Church, St Stephen's Avenue
23. Holy Trinity Church, Westbury-on-Trym
24. Bristol Cathedral, College Green
25. St Mary Redcliffe Church, Redcliffe
26. St Werburgh's Church, St Werburgh's
27. St Paul's Church, St Paul's
28. St Mary Magdalene, Stoke Bishop
29. Holy Trinity Church, Old Market
30. St Thomas the Martyr, Redcliffe
31. St Mary's Church, Shirehampton
32. Church of St Mary the Virgin, Henbury
33. St Alban's Church, Westbury Park
34. Redland Church, Redland
35. The Chapel of the Three Kings of Cologne, Colston Street

Introduction

Bristol has long been known as the 'city of churches'. There are churches with steeples and spires that appear to be reaching for the sky, churches with bell towers ringing out loud and clear above the sound of traffic trundling around the town, and churches with impressive flying buttresses gracefully supporting a heavy roof.

Churches of Bristol looks at some of the city's places of worship – ancient, modern, large and small (the smallest, by the way, measures just 22 × 18 feet). This book tells the fascinating stories of how they were built, along with some of the city's colourful history – for both are intertwined. When it comes to churches, Bristol is certainly different from any other English city or town. The city council is the only local authority in the country to own a church where services are still held.

The foundation date of some churches is unclear, but archaeological excavations show that some of the present buildings stand on sites where Celts, Saxons and Normans once worshipped. History tells us that by the time the explorer John Cabot made his epic voyage from Bristol to America in 1497 there were nineteen parish churches ready to ring out a farewell tune.

This book does not set out to be an academic tome, nor is it a chronological or a definitive history of every church in the city. That would be impossible for a book of this size. It is packed, though, with fascinating facts, such as why various churches were built in certain places, and interesting stories, like the one about the mayor who climbed the highest church spire in the city to mark the end of its reconstruction.

This book tells of how Bristol has played an important part in church history, not just locally but globally. For instance, it was here that the first Methodist chapel in the world was built by John Wesley, the founder of Methodism. It was in Bristol Cathedral that another 'religious first' made headlines around the world: the cathedral hosted the controversial ordination of the first women into the Church of England priesthood. The Bishop of Bristol laid his hands on the heads of thirty-two women and blessed them. This was a service witnessed by hundreds of friends and supporters in the congregation and no doubt by thousands more via the medium of television and radio broadcasts.

During the nineteenth century there was a surge in church building to cope with Bristol's increasing population. The first national census in England in 1801 showed that the city's population was around 63,000. It rose to 154,000 by the time of the 1861 census. Often, people moving into a newly built suburb would appeal to the church authorities for a place of worship to be built near their homes.

Churchgoing in Bristol, especially in Victorian and Edwardian times, was such a focal point of family life that it prompted the *Western Daily Press*, a morning newspaper, to conduct a census of church attendance. It was such a comprehensive survey that it not only included Church of England and Roman Catholic worshippers but also those belonging to lesser-known faiths, like the Swedenborgian Church and the Christadelphians. Also included were those at the Red, White and Blue Temperance Army and Welsh Calvinistic services. The Seamen's Church, a long-derelict building on the edge of the city docks, also took part in the census. When church leaders reported their attendances to the *Western Daily Press* the paper was able to tell its readers that a total of 109,452 people went to church in Bristol on 30 October 1881. The largest congregation was reported to be at St Paul's Church, in the suburb of Southville, where there was a total of 2,316 worshippers at services throughout the day. The paper reported that the vicar was absent on the day of the census, and therefore the number of people in church was possibly less than normal. The only other church that took part in the census and had more than 2,000 people attending its morning and evening services was St Andrew's Parish Church, Clifton, which no longer exists.

Visitors to Bristol are often surprised that the ruins of some churches bombed in the Second World War are still standing. They have been kept as a memorial to civilians who died during the war. Many churches were totally destroyed during the war – some of them during the first major air raid on the city – while scores of others were badly damaged. After that first big raid, which started on a Sunday evening and went on until the early hours of the next day, the Lord Mayor, Alderman Thomas Underdown, described the scene by saying that the 'city of churches' had in one night become 'the city of ruins'. Some churches were rebuilt, while the rubble of others was cleared away and the land sold; for example, one church in Clifton, St Anselm's, was never rebuilt and a health centre now stands on its site. A plaque commemorating the church is fixed to an interior wall of the health centre. St Anselm's was built to ease overcrowding at other nearby Anglican churches. In October 1944 the Bishop of Bristol appealed for £200,000 to be raised in seven years to help with the restoration of churches throughout the diocese of Bristol that had suffered war damage.

On a lighter note, church curiosities are not overlooked in this book. A church in Clifton has a replica standing in a suburb of Shanghai in China. Then there is the city centre church that had an hourglass installed close to the pulpit to ensure that the preacher delivering the sermon didn't speak for too long! Where there wasn't what might be termed a 'proper church' local people met in one of the rooms in a Georgian manor house. The room had been consecrated so that services could be held there. There were also churches where people paid to pray. This was a system known at the time as 'pew mongering'. Families renting a pew gave the church finances a much-needed boost.

Readers may be confused by the various mentions in this book of mayor and lord mayor. Bristol had a mayor from 1216 until 1898 when Queen Victoria bestowed the title of lord mayor on Sir Herbert Ashman, making him the city's 'first' citizen.

No book on Bristol churches would be complete without an account of St Mary Redcliffe, arguably the city's most famous place of worship. Queen Elizabeth I is reputed to have described it as the 'Fairest, goodliest and most famous parish church in the land', though no evidence has ever been found to support this.

Churches of Bristol is a celebration of some of the city's most historic and intriguing churches. I hope that you find nuggets of fascinating information on every page of the book.

1. Church of St James Priory, The Horsefair

Hemmed in by Bristol's bus and coach station and modern office blocks and hotels is St James' Church, parts of which date back to the twelfth century. It claims to be the oldest church in Bristol still in daily use. The church also has the distinction of being the city's oldest building. Of course, when the church was founded in 1129 by Robert Fitzroy, the Earl of Gloucester it was outside Bristol's boundary wall. It is now well inside the civic boundary and stands at the heart of the city and county of Bristol.

The church was part of a Benedictine priory that the earl had set up and was a cell of Tewkesbury Abbey, Gloucestershire. The monks who lived at the monastery reserved the choir and chancel of St James' for themselves but permitted the parishioners to use the nave as a parish church. A tower was added in the fourteenth century at the request of the parishioners, who paid for it. Local legend

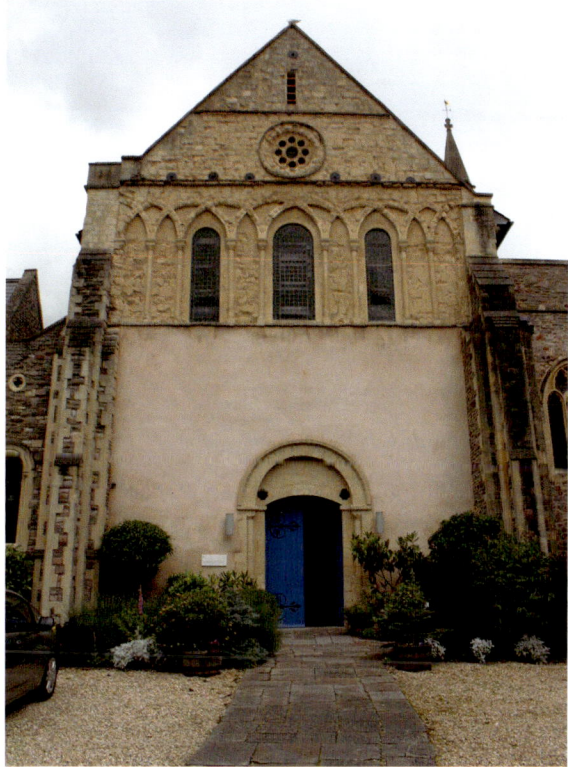

St James' Priory, the oldest of Bristol's churches. (Courtesy of Trevor Naylor)

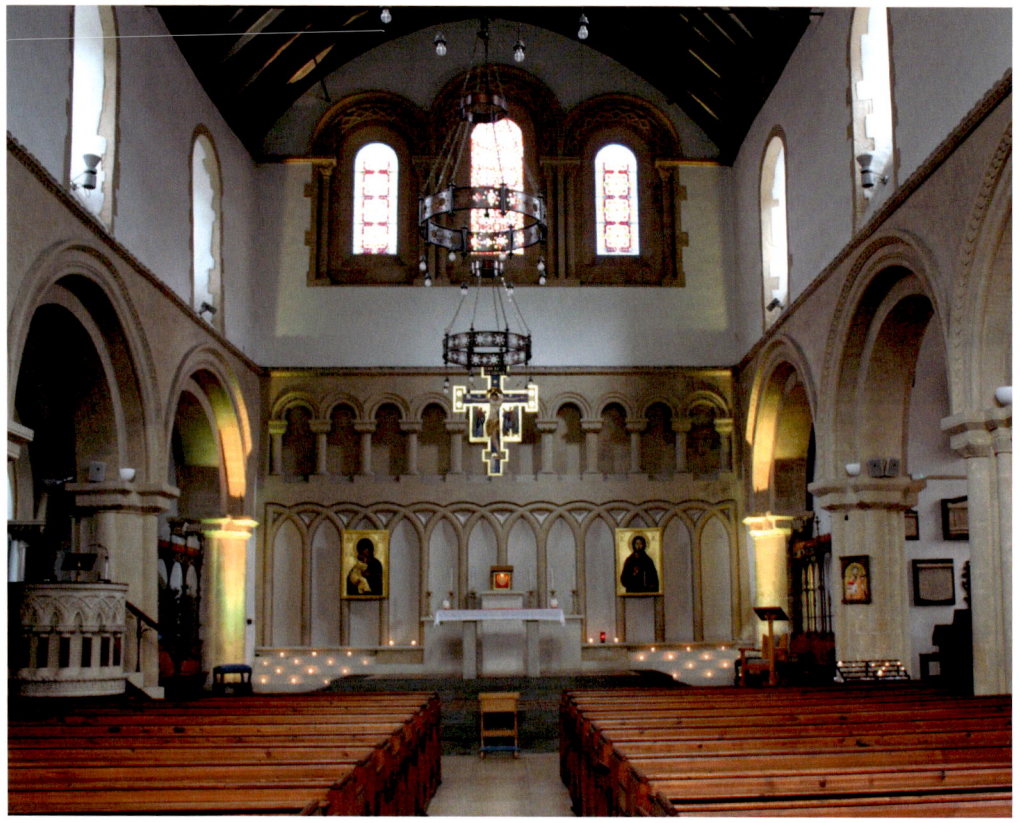

St James' Priory artwork. (Courtesy of Trevor Naylor)

has it that for every tenth stone shipped from Caen in France for the construction of Bristol Castle, the earl ordered that one stone should be set aside for the priory.

The priory was so vast in size that it stretched from what we know today as the Broadmead shopping centre in the south to the residential suburb of Kingsdown in the north. It included churches, a chapter house, cloisters, refectory, cemetery, a gatehouse and gardens. A large stone cross stood in the middle of this ecclesiastical complex. The monks who lived at the monastery were considered the 'social services' for the nearby community.

St James Priory played a part in Bristol's history when Princess Eleanor of Brittany was buried there in 1241. She had been held prisoner in Bristol Castle by her brother King John, thus preventing her from producing an heir to the English throne and threatening his dynasty. The princess was later reburied in Amesbury Abbey, Wiltshire.

During the Dissolution of the Monasteries, most of the priory buildings (except for the parish church) were destroyed under the orders of King Henry VIII. Repairs, alterations and additions have been made to the church over time. St James' Church contains several building styles from the Norman era onwards. The building is thought to have the oldest wheel window in the country, which can easily be seen from the outside. Below the window are three round-headed Norman windows surrounded by interlacing arches. Meanwhile, the south aisle was widened in the late seventeenth century. The church is designated as a Grade I listed building because of its 'exceptional architectural and historic interest'.

In the eighteenth century, John and Charles Wesley, ordained Anglican ministers and founders of the Methodist Church, considered St James' to be their parish church and often preached there.

In 1984, with many people having moved out of the parish, the church was declared redundant and closed. In 2009 the Heritage Lottery Fund granted it more than £3 million for restoration, especially for repairs to the leaking roof. After a substantial conservation and restoration programme, the church was reopened to the public.

St James' Church today is an active church within the Roman Catholic diocese of Clifton. Meanwhile, the St James Priory Project is the charity that has responsibility for the church building. It also operates St James House, which supports on-site housing accommodation for those in recovery from addiction.

It is said that the priory's founder had the church in mind as his final resting place. A tomb dedicated to Robert Fitzroy can be found in a corner of the nave, although there has been some debate among historians as to whether he was ever laid to rest there or if the tomb was a later memorial.

2. The New Room or Wesley's Chapel, The Horsefair

Bristol plays an extremely important part in the history of Methodism, for it was in this city that its founder John Wesley built the first Methodist chapel in the world. He did so shortly after arriving in Bristol in the spring of 1739. He was inspired to do so by the large congregations that gathered to hear his open-air sermons. John Wesley bought a plot of land at The Horsefair and built the New Room, where the first meetings were held in June 1739. The two-storey building was expanded eleven years later and restored in the early 1930s and refurbished again in modern times. A deed of conveyance dated 29 June 1739 preserved in the offices of Bristol Archives records the sale of these premises: 'Mr. Wesley's New Room' by William Lyne to John Wesley for £53 1s chief rent a year.

The New Room, with its beautifully simple chapel, still stands on its original site, but over the years it has become hemmed in by the growth of the post-war Broadmead shopping centre and is now nestling between large departmental stores. As Wesley's first headquarters, it has become a modern Mecca and attracts thousands of pilgrims from all over the world every year.

The chapel we see today is much the same as it was in 1748, except for the central block of pews. These were built when the building was restored in 1929–31 as copies of the seating introduced by the Welsh Calvinist Methodists, who owned the New Room from 1808 to 1929. The chapel was restored the following year. The original seats were the benches that are on either side of the chapel and in the gallery. Men and women sat separately in those days.

The early Methodists were frequently attacked by mobs. The lack of windows on the ground floor was a safety measure against such attacks. The building

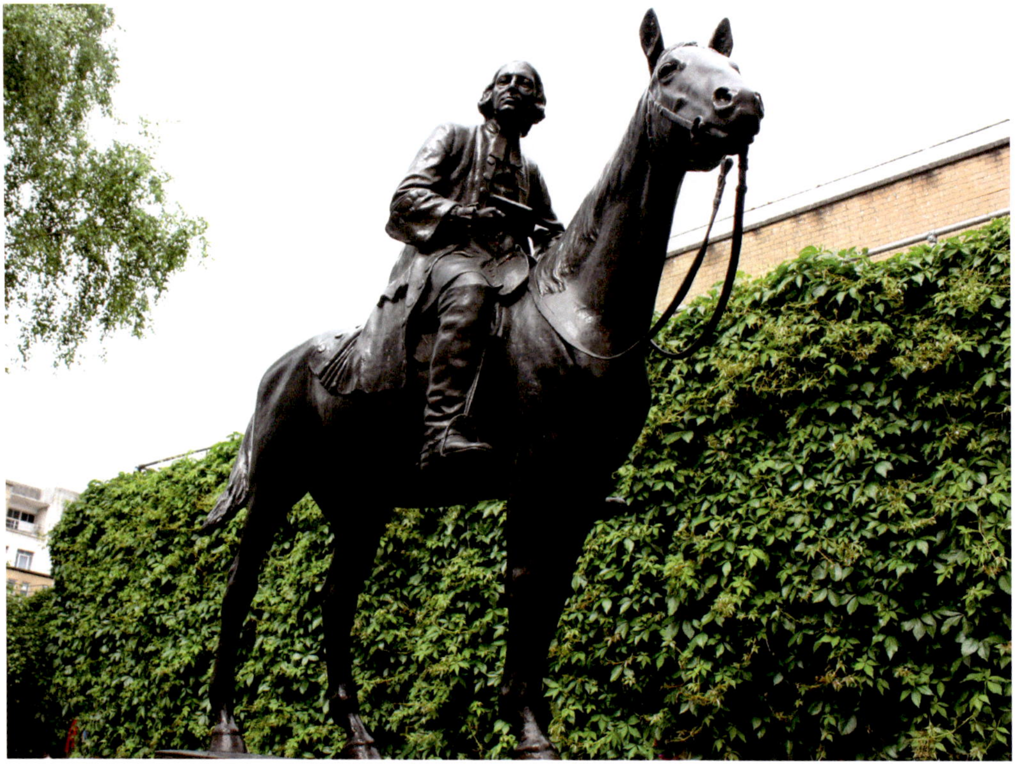

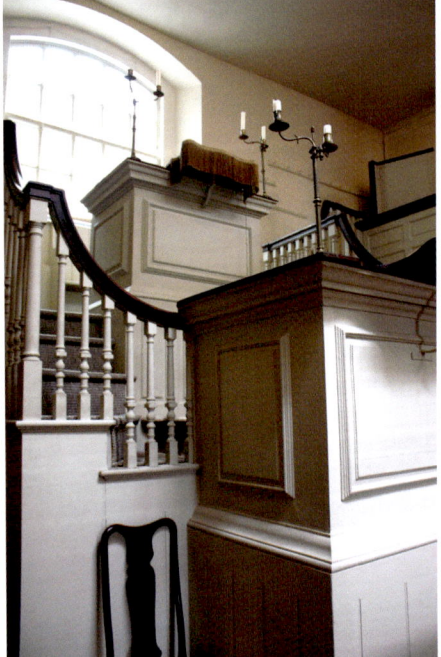

Above: John Wesley on horseback outside Methodist New Room. (Courtesy of Trevor Naylor)

Left: Double pulpit in Methodist New Room. (Courtesy of Trevor Naylor)

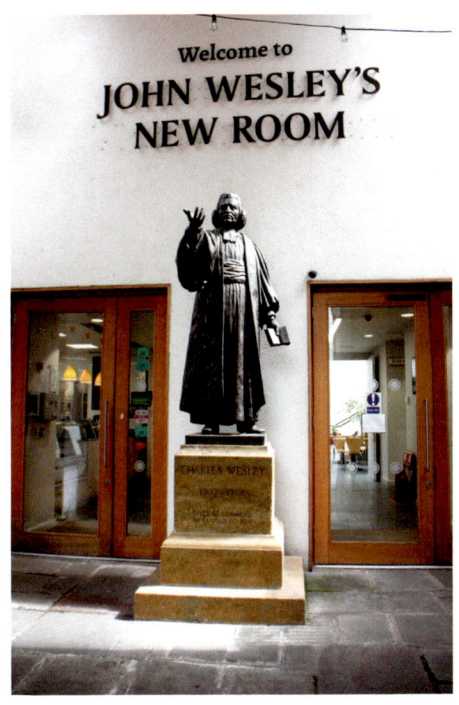
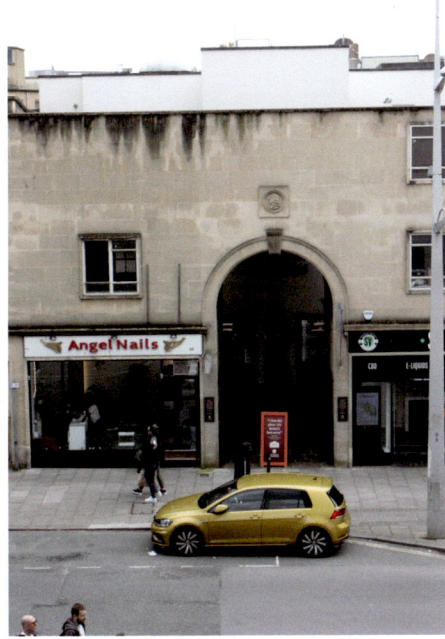

Above left: Statue of Charles Wesley, Methodist New Room. (Courtesy of Trevor Naylor)

Above right: Entrance to Methodist New Room in a modern shopping development. (Courtesy of Trevor Naylor)

Below: Stained glass at Methodist New Room. (Courtesy of Trevor Naylor)

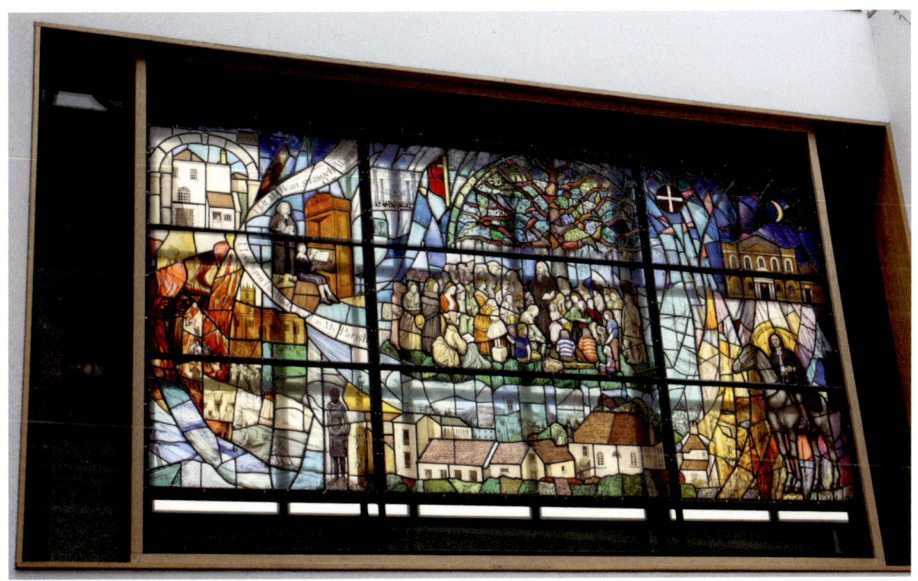

was also designed so that it was difficult for any mob that broke in to reach the preacher quickly, hence the limited access upstairs.

A most unusual feature of the New Room is its double-decker pulpit. The top pulpit was used by the preachers while the lower one was occupied by the person delivering readings from the Bible and conducting other parts of the service. Above the chapel are twelve rooms where John Wesley and his visiting preachers stayed when they were in Bristol. The rooms now house a museum telling the life stories of John and his hymn-writing brother Charles, as well as reflecting on the relevance of Methodism past and present. Besides being used for worship, the New Room was also used as a dispensary and schoolrooms for the poor of the area.

Preaching services took place in the mornings, beginning as early as 5 a.m., and sometimes in the evenings too. The New Room still has the Communion table at which John and Charles Wesley celebrated the Lord's Supper. Sometimes there were special services including 'Watch-night' services, which lasted overnight till dawn.

Not far from the New Room is the site where John Wesley preached his first open-air sermon a couple of days after arriving in Bristol. It was at a brickyard at St Philips, which is said to have been packed with some 3,000 people. Wesley's last open-air meeting was also held in Bristol. In the intervening years he is believed to have travelled an estimated 250,000 miles on horseback to preach something like 40,000 sermons all over the country. A reminder of this equestrian feat is a bronze statue of John Wesley sat astride a horse in the forecourt of the New Room. Another statue, this time of his brother, stands in the rear courtyard.

The Church of England regarded John Wesley as being too revolutionary and banned him from many of its pulpits. However, John Wesley got around this ruling when he was invited to preach at the Lord Mayor's Chapel, which was under the jurisdiction of Bristol Corporation.

3. St Peter's Church, Castle Park

It is hard to believe that the large, open, green space in the centre of the city we know as Castle Park was the site of Bristol Castle until it was destroyed on the instructions of Oliver Cromwell (Lord Protector of England) in 1654. Close to the castle stood Bristol's first church. It was dedicated to St Peter and was built during the Norman era. Today only its roofless and windowless walls and its tower, 79 feet high to the base of its pinnacles, remain. The only parts of the Norman structure that have survived are the lower parts of the tower. St Peter's was gutted during the first major air raid on Bristol in the Second World War. This was on the night of Sunday 24/25 November 1940. It is said that the vicar of St Peter's heard an air-raid siren warning of an imminent attack, and therefore cut short the evening service and sent his congregation home early.

By the twentieth century, streets around the church, which stood in Peter Street, were packed with shops, many of them branches of national stores. This was Bristol's main shopping centre. Both the church and nearby shops were reduced to piles of twisted girders and ashes in that first big air raid, when incendiary bombs and high-explosive bombs were dropped by the German Luftwaffe. More than

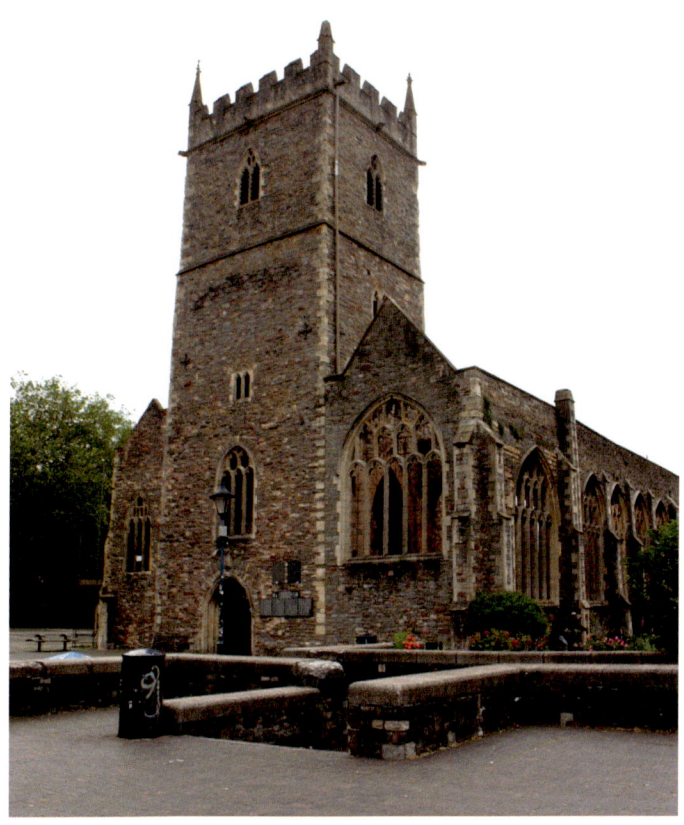

Derelict St Peter's Church in Castle Park. (Courtesy of Trevor Naylor)

200 people lost their lives in Bristol that night. During the war Bristol suffered a total of seventy-seven air raids, making it the fifth heaviest-bombed city in the country.

Internal fixtures of St Peter's Church were destroyed and memorials, including one of a former mayor, were badly damaged. Alderman Thomas Underdown, who was lord mayor of Bristol at the time, said: 'The city of churches had in one night become the city of ruins.' The ruins of St Peter's Church have been preserved by Bristol City Council as a war memorial. A plaque has been fixed to an exterior wall commemorating 'civilians and auxiliary personnel from the Greater Bristol area who lost their lives in the war between June 1940 and May 1944'. Some of them were firemen, air-raid wardens and police officers. Their names all appear on the plaque.

Little information is known about St Peter's Church in its early days. Records do show that it underwent major repairs several times in the eighteenth century, however. Archaeologists who have carried out excavations amid the ruins of St Peter's Church are almost certain that it stands on the site of an Anglo-Saxon place of worship,

English Heritage has designated the church ruins as a Grade II* listed building. It also stands in a conservation area.

4. St Mary Le Port, Castle Park

The church of St Mary Le Port, on the north-west edge of Castle Park, was in use until it was burnt out in 1940 when it was heavily bombed in the war. Internal fixtures, like memorials to prominent citizens, were either destroyed or badly damaged. The majority of the church walls were later demolished, leaving only the tower standing to its full height of 72 feet to the base of its pinnacles. At one time the churchyard extended to the river and there was a mooring post for ships. Excavations in the twentieth century by archaeologists have revealed that the church was originally built in a thriving industrial area in the late Saxon and early medieval periods. Saxon pottery was found nearby. The church was rebuilt between the eleventh and fifteenth centuries. Its tower is fifteenth century and was built in the Perpendicular architectural style. St Mary Le Port Street, in which the church stood, no longer exists.

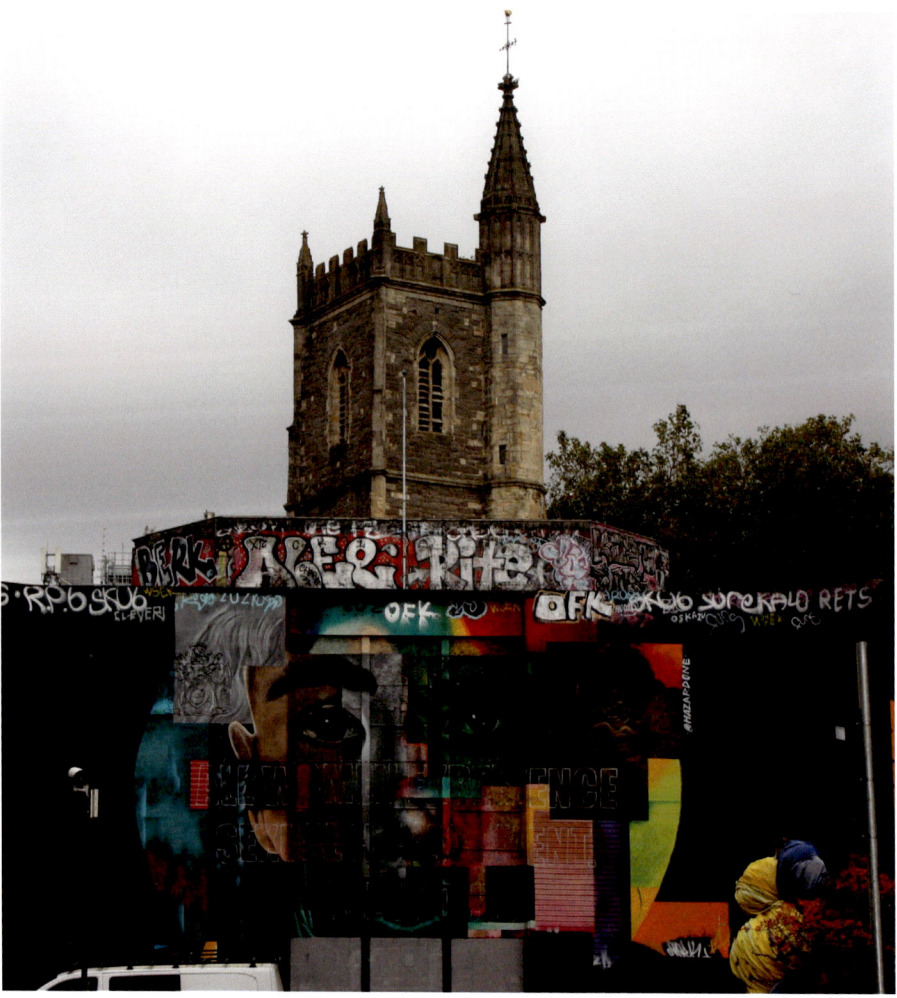

Ruins of St Mary Le Port behind derelict commercial buildings. (Courtesy of Trevor Naylor)

A lot of the church's records were destroyed in the Blitz, but ancient deeds show that it was styled as St Mary de Foro or St Mary of the Market. The word 'port' is derived from the Latin *porto*, meaning a market town.

A saint with a rather strange background was remembered by congregations at St Mary Le Port. A chapel and an altar in the church were dedicated to St Wilgefortis. She was also known as St Uncumber and was the patron saint of unhappily married women. Apparently, she had taken a vow of chastity and is said to have grown a beard to cover her beauty in the hope that this would put off men who might contemplate marrying her. The cult of St Wilgefortis was extremely popular in late medieval Europe, but she may well have been one of those saints who never existed.

The tower of St Mary Le Port is both a Grade II listed building and a Scheduled Ancient Monument. Human remains in the churchyard have been removed to Canford Cemetery at Westbury-on-Trym. For some years now a large section of the tower has been obscured by derelict boarded-up office blocks that surround it. One of the office blocks housed the regional branch of the Bank of England. Plans have been announced to transform the derelict area, which would reveal the tower and ruins around it. These plans include new shops, offices, improved landscaping of Castle Park. Long-demolished medieval roads like St Mary Le Port Street would also be reinstated.

The towers of St Peter's and St Mary Le Port have long been a headache for Bristol City Council. For many years after the Second World War negotiations between the council and church authorities dragged on. Eventually the towers changed hands for a total of £93,650. On top of this, there were further costs for making each tower safe.

5. St John the Baptist, Broad Street

Despite its name, Broad Street is quite a narrow thoroughfare. It is one of the city's oldest roads, with buildings of various periods and styles of architecture and an ancient church at each end. At the bottom of Broad Street, leading off the city centre, is one of Bristol's least-altered medieval churches. It is also one of the smallest places of worship in the city, consisting of a nave and chancel divided by a pointed arch.

The present building was founded on the site of a place of worship dating to around 1388. The church of St John the Baptist is unique in that it stands astride the only survivor of the nine portcullised gateways in Bristol, which led through the city wall in the Middle Ages – hence it is popularly known as St John's on the Arch or St John's on the Wall. Its floor plan was constrained by its location along the line of the city wall. Its narrow nave is the thickness of that wall.

The city wall, with its gateways, was often the site of religious processions and pageants, which were staged to welcome notable visitors to Bristol. It was through St John's Gateway that Queen Elizabeth I entered the city on a white horse on one of her royal progresses around her realm in 1574.

Unusually, the church has no east or west windows. Natural light is provided by the Perpendicular windows in the side walls, which happen to be in two different streets.

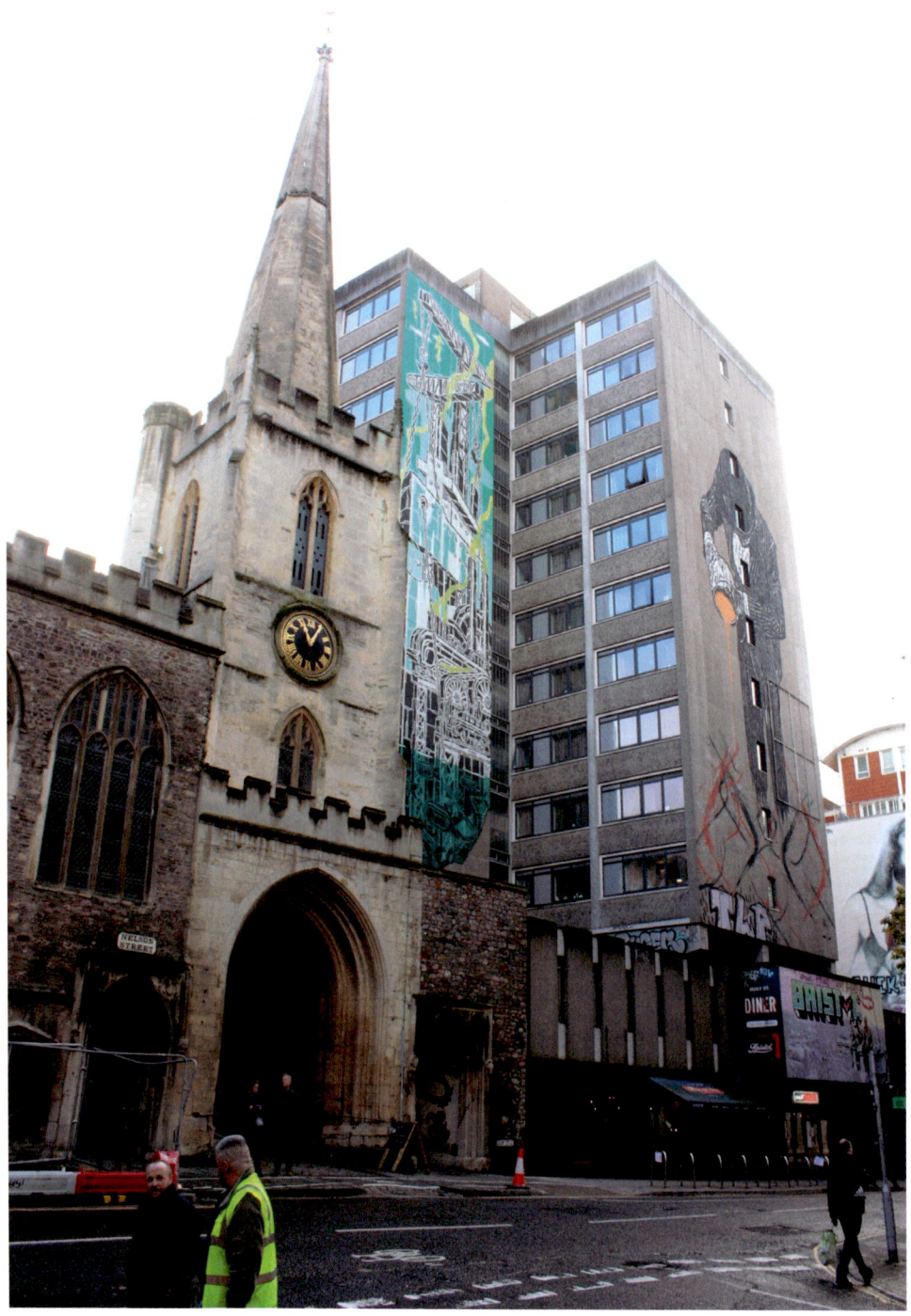

St John's on the Arch surrounded by modern commercial buildings. (Courtesy of Trevor Naylor)

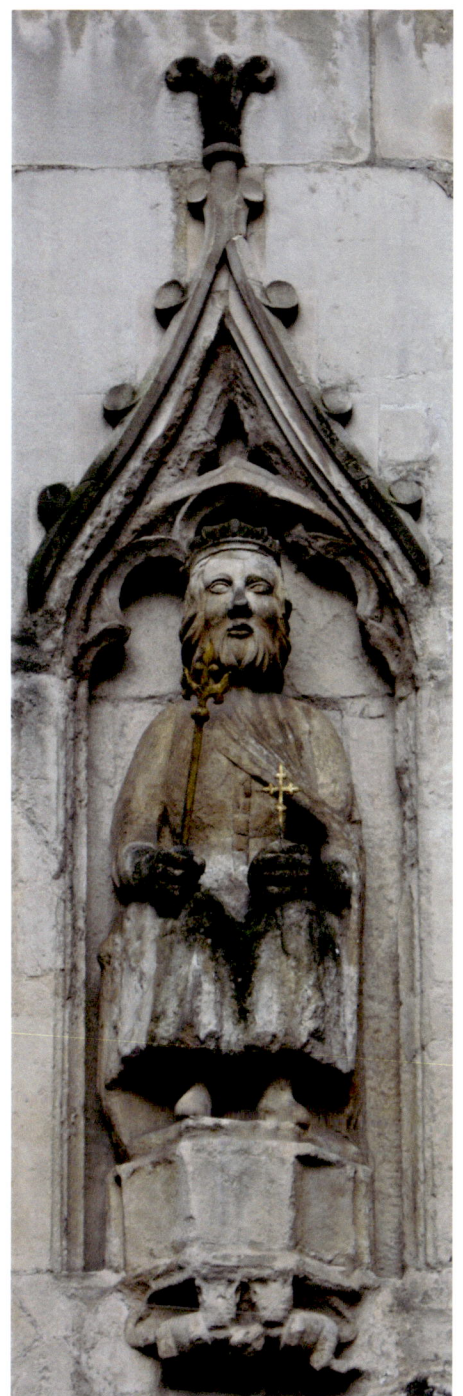 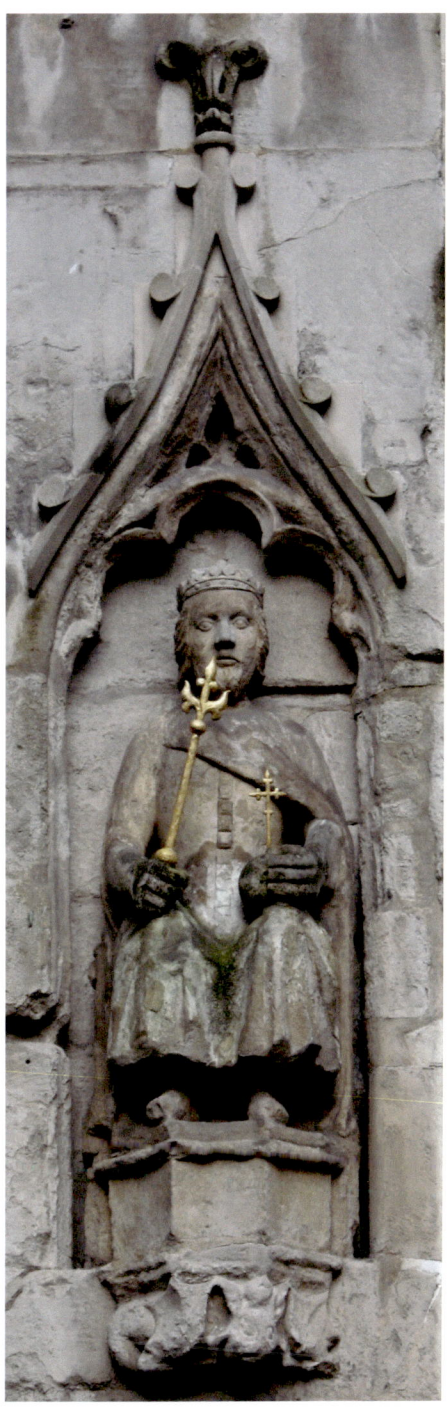

Above left and above right: Statues of Brennus and Belinus, mythical founders of Bristol, on St John's Arch. (Courtesy of Trevor Naylor)

The present church was founded by a wealthy businessman, Walter Frampton, in the fourteenth century. He was mayor of Bristol three times. His effigy lies on a tomb-chest in the chancel.

By the side of the octagonal pulpit stood an hourglass designed to prevent the preacher delivering lengthy sermons. The hourglass has long been in the safe keeping of Bristol Museum. Few people know that in the nineteenth century the church crypt was used as an engine house and later as a sugar warehouse; during the Second World War it became an air-raid shelter.

Standing in niches on either side of the central arch of the city wall are two statues purporting to be those of Brennus and Belinus, Roman soldiers who were supposed to have founded Bristol. Both men are holding an orb and a sceptre. No one knows who carved these now weather-beaten statues or installed them on the arch, although they probably first appeared in the fifteenth century.

When the nearby church of St Mary Le Port on the edge of Castle Park was gutted in the Second World War, its congregation moved to St John the Baptist Church. However, when the number of worshippers dwindled, St John's was declared redundant as a place of worship. It is now in the care of the Churches Conservation Trust and is available for hire for performance or as an exhibition space.

6. Temple Church, Temple Way

The most notable feature of Temple Church, apart from its wartime ruins, is its leaning tower – a local landmark. It is often referred to as Bristol's answer to the Leaning Tower of Pisa. It looks as though the tower is going to topple down at any moment onto the much smaller shops and public house near its base. However, the tower, which is 5 feet out of true, has been like this for more than 500 years. This peculiarity is believed to have been first mentioned in 1568 when the Duke of Norfolk visited Bristol. It had become a custom to show visitors that a stone as large as an egg thrust into a chink between the tower and the church wall would be crushed to powder when the bells were rung. The duke was a witness to this experiment.

Work on building the tower started in the fourteenth century, but during its construction the foundations sank. It is supposed to have been built as far up as the first two stages upon wooden piles, which gradually sank as the weight increased. Efforts were made to bring the 113-foot-high tower back into a more upright position, but they were unsuccessful.

It was on this site that the first Temple Church was built. It was a round or oval shrine of the Knights Templar, an order of soldier-monks who guarded the roads to Jerusalem during the Crusades. They proudly wore white habits on top of their armour that had a red cross emblazoned on them. Their church in Bristol was named Temple Church, or the Church of the Holy Cross, and is believed to have been built in the twelfth century. During the fourteenth century it became a parish church and was rebuilt into a rectangular shape. One of the interesting features of the church was the Weavers' Chapel, which was set apart for the use of the ancient Guild of Weavers, many of whom lived in the area around the church.

Temple Church was destroyed by incendiary bombs during the air raid of 24/25 November 1940. Only the shell of the church has been left standing along

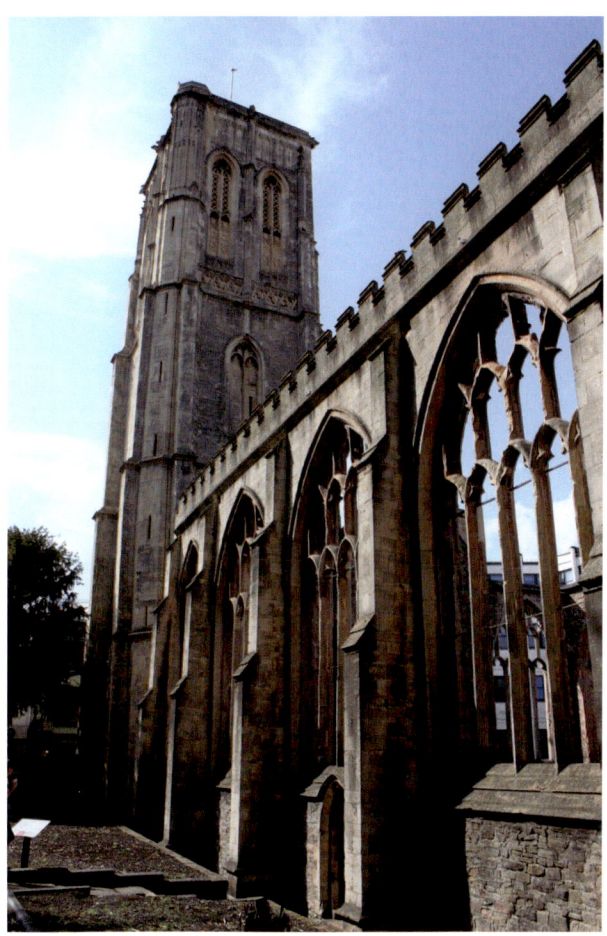

Temple Church, Bristol's answer to the Leaning Tower of Pisa. (Courtesy of Trevor Naylor)

with the tower. Many internal fixtures that were saved (though slightly damaged) were given to other churches after the bombing raid, such as a peal of eight bells given to Bristol Cathedral which hang in its north-west tower.

The tower of Temple Church, which is close to Temple Meads rail station, is not open for viewing, but the remains of its main building can easily be seen at close-up.

A story is often recounted that a soldier from the Royal Engineers had to be dissuaded from demolishing the tower on the grounds of safety. He believed that enemy action in the Second World War had made it a dangerous building.

Temple Church is owned by the diocese of Bristol, although it is in the care of English Heritage. The church is designated as a Grade II* listed building.

7. Christ Church with St Ewen, Broad Street

At the top end of Broad Street stands Christ Church with St Ewen, which escaped destruction in the Second World War. A popular theory is that the thickness of its walls saved it from destruction.

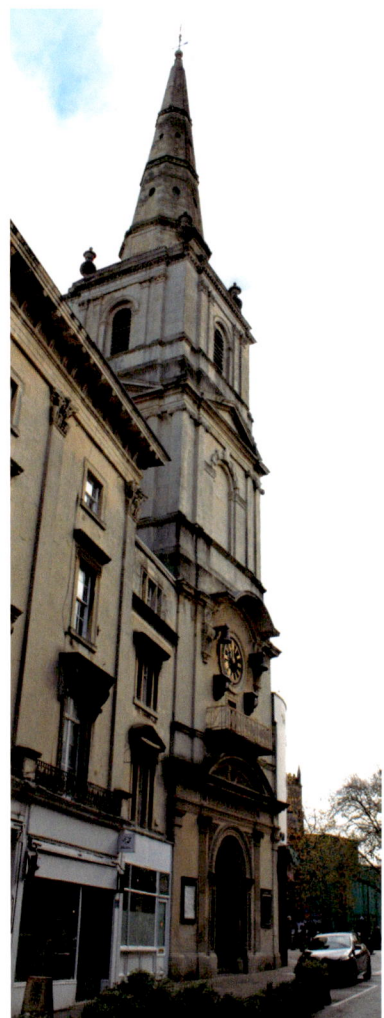 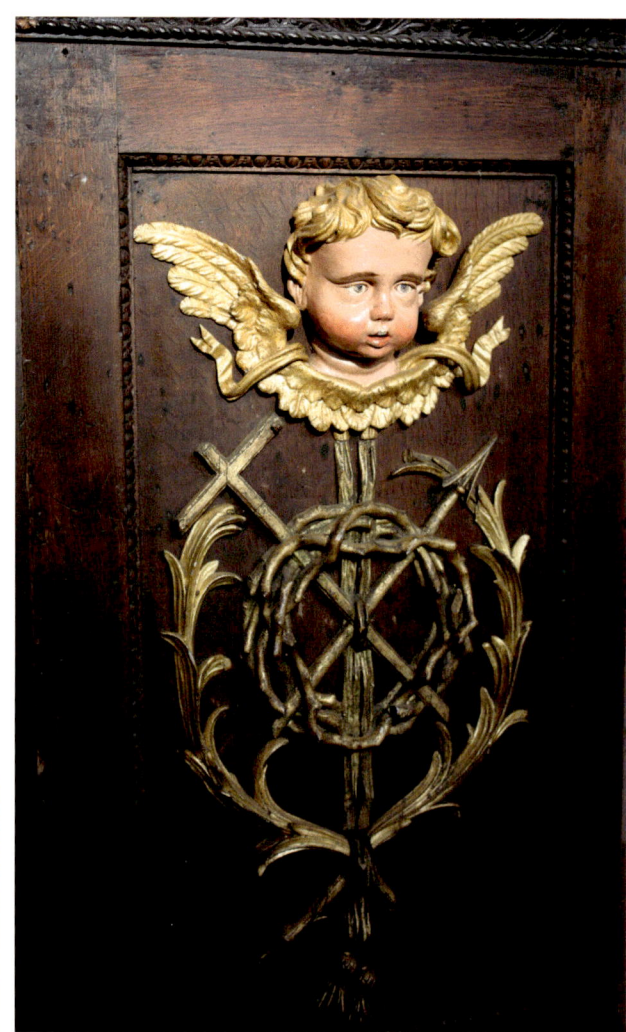

Above left: Christ Church, Broad Street. (Courtesy of Trevor Naylor)

Above right: Pulpit discarded in Victorian times and now restored in Christ Church. (Courtesy of Trevor Naylor)

Opposite: Interior view of Christ Church. (Courtesy of Trevor Naylor)

Christ Church stands near the site of the High Cross, which was built to celebrate Bristol becoming the first county outside London in 1373. It was built between 1786 and 1791 and is often regarded as the city's finest church of the eighteenth-century classical period. It is the third church on this site, which is at the heart of the old city. The present building was constructed by Thomas Paty & Sons and is believed to be the third Christ Church on the same site. The Paty family of builders, architects and masons have often been described as the 'makers

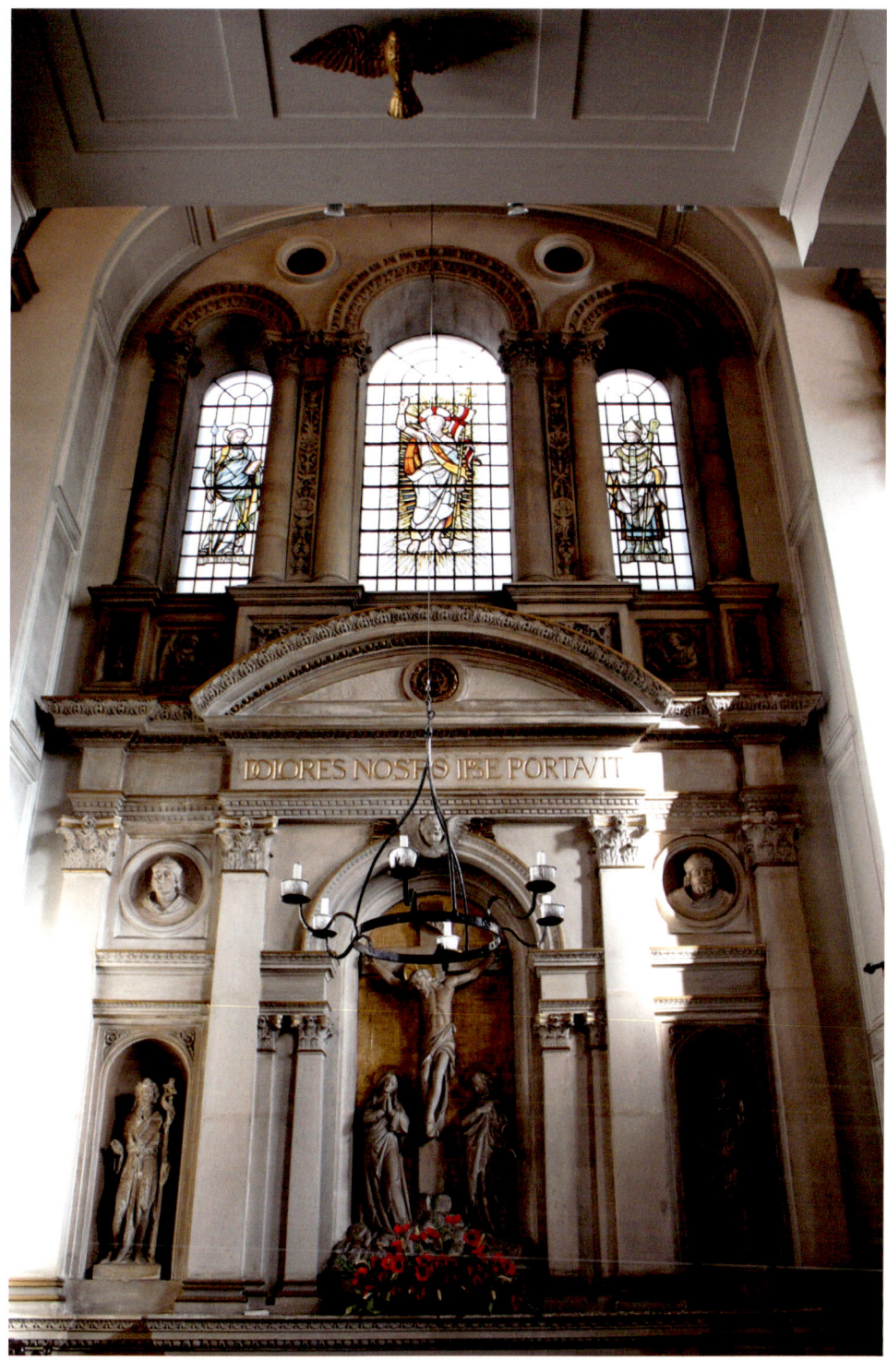

of eighteenth-century Bristol'. They were the foremost designers and craftsmen of their time in the city.

The tower of Christ Church contains a peal of ten bells and its spire is 160 feet high. Below the nave is a fairly spacious crypt. The church's elegant interior, with its Corinthian columns and rood screen, was the work of William Paty. One of the many memorials in the church to distinguished local residents is signed by Thomas Paty.

For more than 350 years two Roman quarter jacks standing on specially built ledges 50 feet above the church porch, one of them either side of the clock, have been a big attraction. The quarter jacks chimed the quarter hours and over the years they attracted large audiences of not only church visitors but judges, barristers and solicitors working in the law courts on the opposite side of Broad Street. The quarter jacks were taken down in 2013 for restoration, but the brightly painted wooden figures were found to be in such a poor state that they could not be used outside the church again. They have since been put into the care of Bristol Museum.

The Baptismal Register of Christ Church for 1774 contains the name 'Robert Southey'. As a youngster he lived in Wine Street, around the corner from the church. Southey was appointed Poet Laureate in 1813. In a letter dated 1806, he wrote: 'There were quarter boys to this old church clock … and I have many a time stopped with my satchel at my back to see them strike.' The last time the quarter jacks were repaired and painted was early in the 1990s when major work was carried out to the church tower.

St Ewen's Church, founded in the twelfth century, stood opposite Christ Church on the corner of Broad Street and Corn Street. St Ewen's Church was demolished under an Act of Parliament obtained in 1788. It made way for the building that is today known as the Old Council House and is home to Bristol Register Office. After the demolition, St Ewen's parish was united with that of Christ Church.

8. Hope Chapel, Hotwells

When Lady Henrietta Hope visited the Hotwells natural spa she left her mark on the area by founding a chapel which, more than two centuries later, is still being used for prayer and praise. Lady Hope, whose home was near Edinburgh, travelled around the United Kingdom with her friend Viscountess Glenorchy. Both were taking the waters for healthy living. The couple arrived at Hotwells in 1785 when the spa was enjoying its heyday with visitors, including various overseas royalty such as Queen Catherine of Braganza.

One of Lady Hope's keen interests was that of promoting the cause of religion, and she endowed a number of churches around the United Kingdom. Lady Hope and her friend searched the Hotwells area for a suitable plot of land on which they could build a chapel for Calvinistic evangelic worship. The couple eventually settled on a steep hill rising from Hotwells up to Clifton, which eventually became known as Hope Chapel Hill. Unfortunately, Lady Hope died on New Year's Day in 1786 before work on a church building could start. She left £2,500 in her will towards the cost of the project.

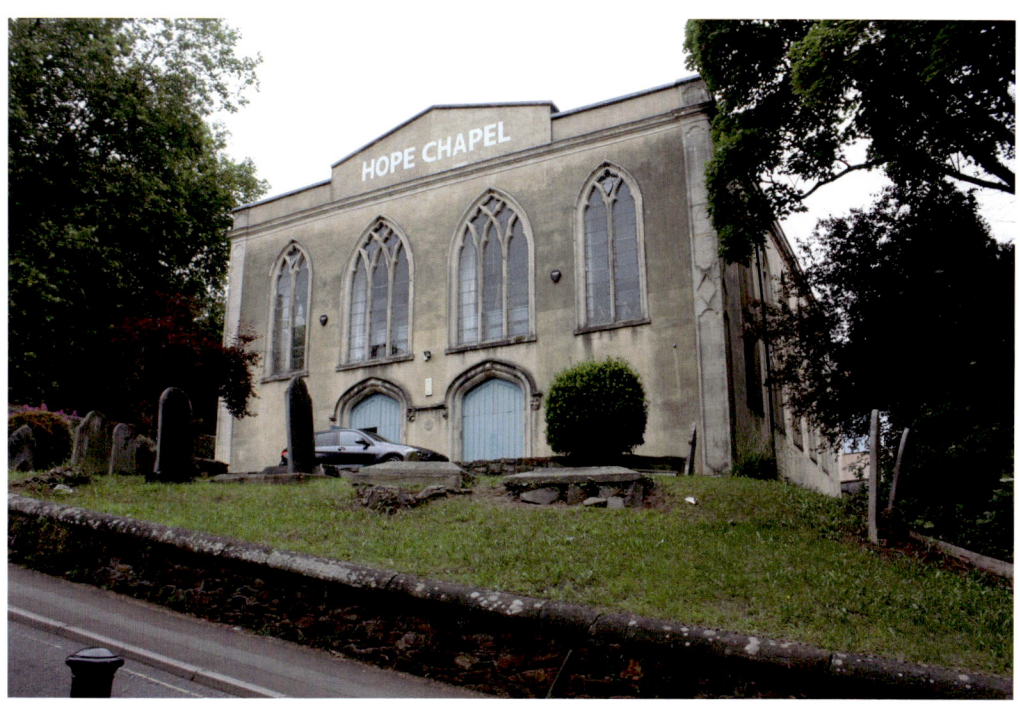

Above: Hope Chapel, Hotwells. (Courtesy of Trevor Naylor)

Below: Hope Chapel, now a multi-use space. (Courtesy of Trevor Naylor)

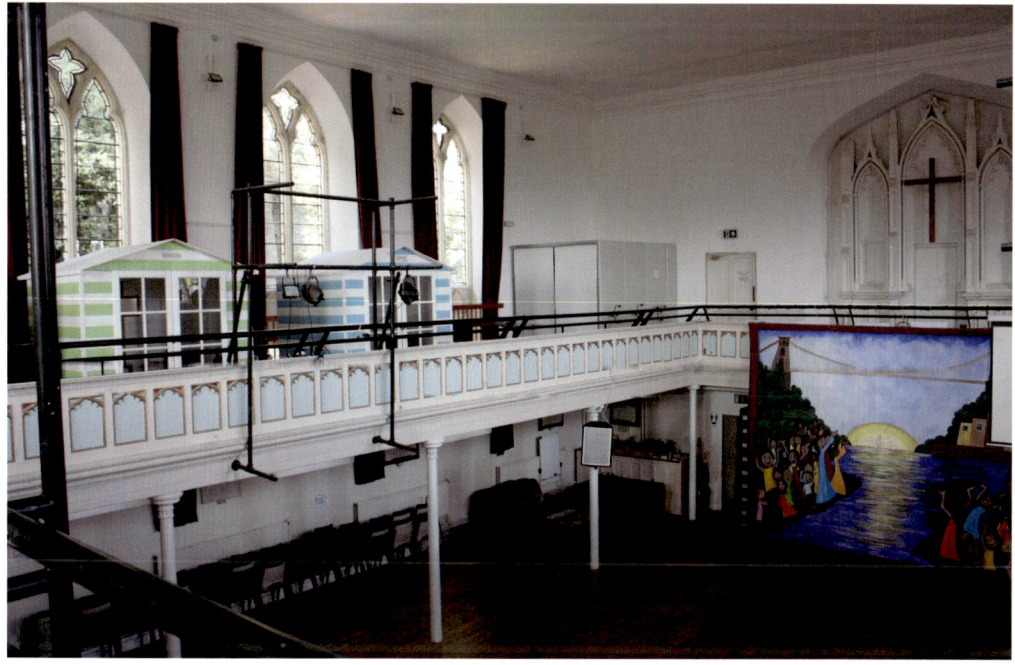

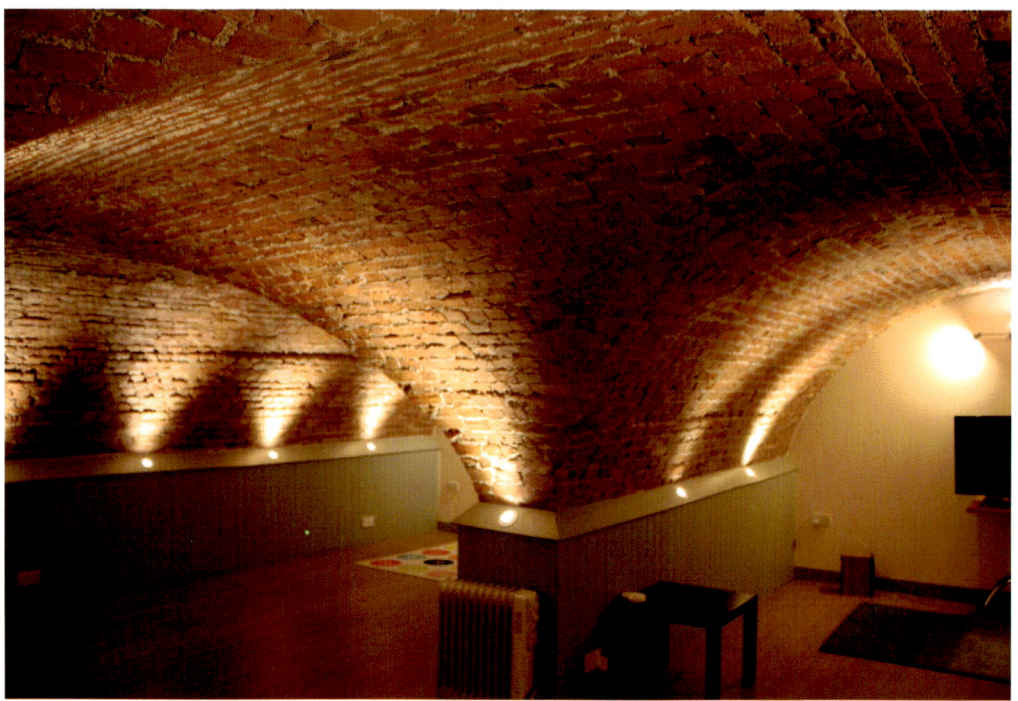

Hope Chapel crypt. (Courtesy of Trevor Naylor)

Lady Glenorchy, who had also founded several chapels in Scotland, started to make her friend's wish come true. However, she too did not live long enough to see the chapel completed. That task was left to her executors.

Hope Chapel, aptly named after its founder, was ready for its first service in August 1788. It is one of the oldest free (from the establishment) churches in Bristol. It was built with room for 900 people. It is essentially a hall with a balcony on three sides supported by cast-iron columns. Lady Hope was buried in the vault beneath the chapel.

Visiting Nonconformist ministers and Anglican priests shared the pulpit until a resident minister was appointed in 1820. To cope with the increasing numbers of people moving into Hotwells and Clifton, the chapel was enlarged in 1838. By 1851 around 600 people attended the Sunday morning service; the figure soared by 100 for the evening prayers. However, by the 1980s the congregation had dropped to around a dozen people and the building was in such a state of disrepair that it was closed. After major repair work the building reopened as the home of Hope Community Church, a free church with a regular congregation.

9. Holy Trinity Church, Hotwells Road

Walk down Hope Chapel Hill and turn left into Hotwells Road and you immediately come face to face with Holy Trinity Church, originally a Regency church. Work started on construction in 1829 and it was completed the following

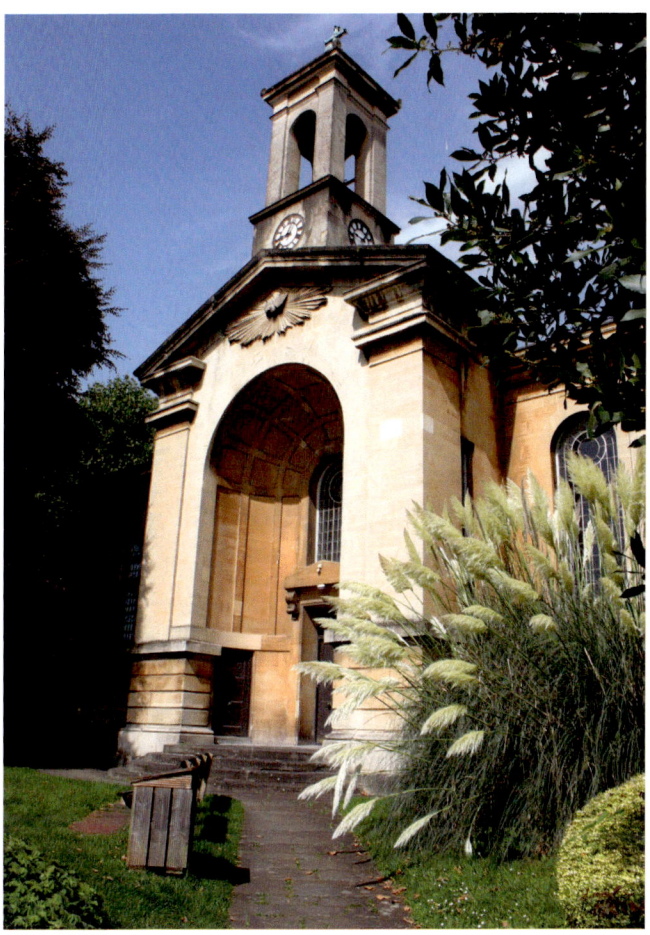

Holy Trinity Church, Hotwells. (Courtesy of Trevor Naylor)

year. It was built with great speed as increasing numbers of people were moving into the Hotwells area. The church had room for 1,654 people.

The church authorities commissioned Professor Charles Cockerell, a leading authority on classical and Renaissance architecture, to design Holy Trinity Church. It was built with large, tiered galleries on three sides and a small hemispherical dome supported by four Doric columns. The church cost around £10,000, with a local benefactor providing approximately £6,000 of the funding.

The interior of Holy Trinity Church was destroyed on the night of 3 January 1941 in one of the many night-time air raids on Bristol during the Second World War. Incendiary bombs landed on the roof and very quickly the church was consumed by fire. Subsequently, the congregation met at the neighbouring church of St Andrew-the-Less in Dowry Square, which has long since been demolished.

After the war, Church of England authorities agreed that a new interior for Holy Trinity Church should be accommodated within the four original walls of Regency style that had been left standing after the air raid. Reconstruction work took place between 1955 and 1958 at a cost of £60,000, most of which was met by the War Damage Commission. There was also financial support from Holy Trinity's parochial church council as well as from a local fundraising campaign. One of the four bells at Holy Trinity Church was lost during the war, but the remaining three were recast into one.

A local newspaper reported that when the church was reconsecrated in 1958 by the Bishop of Malmesbury, some 2,000 people watched the arrival of his procession. In his sermon, the bishop said to a packed church: 'Some people might ask why spend so much money on a building today, when there are so many causes needing financial support?' His answer was that all that had been done in the building was their means of expressing 'the true relationship between God and man'. He said that 'no place can be too lovely and no act of worship too profound'.

In 2023 Holy Trinity Church joined with St Stephen's Church in the city centre to form a single parish benefice known as the City of Bristol Harbourside Churches.

10. ALL SAINTS' CHURCH, CORN STREET

All Saints' Church in the very heart of ancient Bristol can be identified by its imposing classical cupola, which is a prominent landmark in the centre of the city. At one time a steeple stood where the tower now stands. The church was founded in Norman times, although the existing building was partly rebuilt after a fire in 1466.

Formerly known as All Hallows' Church, it is surrounded on three sides by pedestrian passageways and is built into surrounding commercial buildings, so it is seldom noticed by passers-by. The entrance to the church is in the rather narrow All Saints Lane. Its tower, however, stands out on the skyline thanks to the cupola, ball and cross that surmount it. Except for four Norman columns and a font, the interior of the church is in Perpendicular style.

All Saints' is notable for a marble effigy carved by the Flemish sculptor Rysbrach of the Bristol philanthropist and slave trader Edward Colston reclining on his tomb. He has long been lauded for founding schools, an almshouse and making monetary gifts to many churches, including All Saints. It was said that his gifts amounted to £80,000 – a lot of money in Colston's day. A list of his benefactions appears inscribed on a tablet above his tomb. Although Colston died at Mortlake in 1721, his body was brought back to Bristol and interred with great ceremony at midnight.

In days long past, a nosegay of flowers was placed on the Colston monument every Sunday. However, in recent years Colston has lost his lustre because of his involvement with slave trading. He was a member of the Court of Assistants to the London-based Royal Africa Company, which had a monopoly on the slave trade until 1698. A statue of Colston that stood in nearby Colston Avenue, not far from All Saints' Church, was dragged from its plinth, toppled, defaced and pushed into Bristol Harbour during protests related to the Black Lives Matter movement in 2020.

For many years All Saints' Church was used as a Diocesan Education Centre, but it has been closed to the public since 2015.

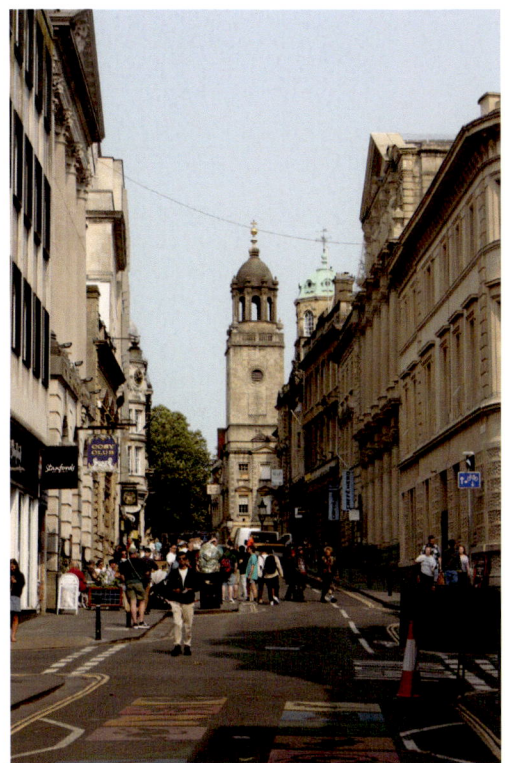 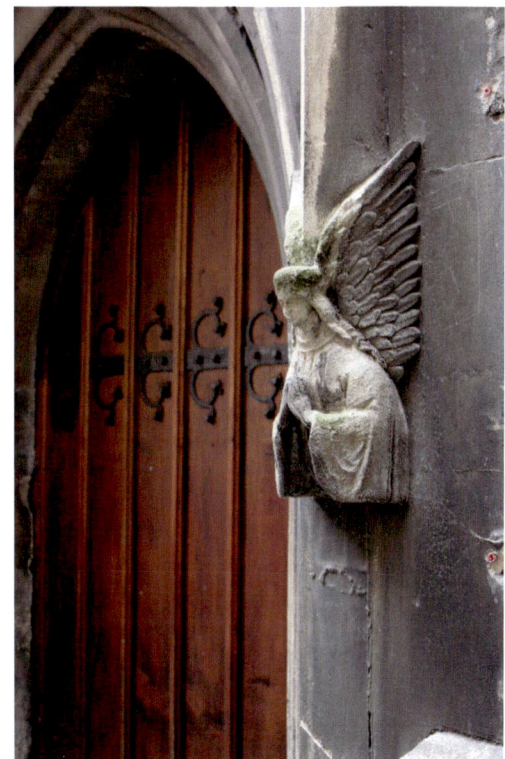

Above left: All Saints' Church, Corn Street. (Courtesy of Trevor Naylor)

Above right: Detail of carving in All Saints' Church, Corn Street. (Courtesy of Trevor Naylor)

11. All Saints' Church, Clifton

It was to meet the spiritual needs of the fast-growing population in Clifton that All Saints' Church in Pembroke Road was founded. The Church of England bought part of a field from the Society of Merchant Venturers, who owned much land and property in the area. An architect of national renown, George Edmund Street, who was probably best known for his design of the Royal Courts of Justice on the Strand in London, produced a design for All Saints' Church in Gothic Revival style. He envisaged that the congregation would have an uninterrupted view of the chancel, pulpit and altar. All Saints' Church was consecrated in 1881, although it consisted of only a brick-built nave.

A census of church attendance in October 1881 carried out by a local newspaper showed that All Saints' Church was one of the most popular places of worship in the city. It was listed as holding six services each Sunday, starting at 6 a.m. At matins the priest ministered to 562 people, while 652 attended the main morning service with a congregation of more than 800 people packing the pews for evening prayers.

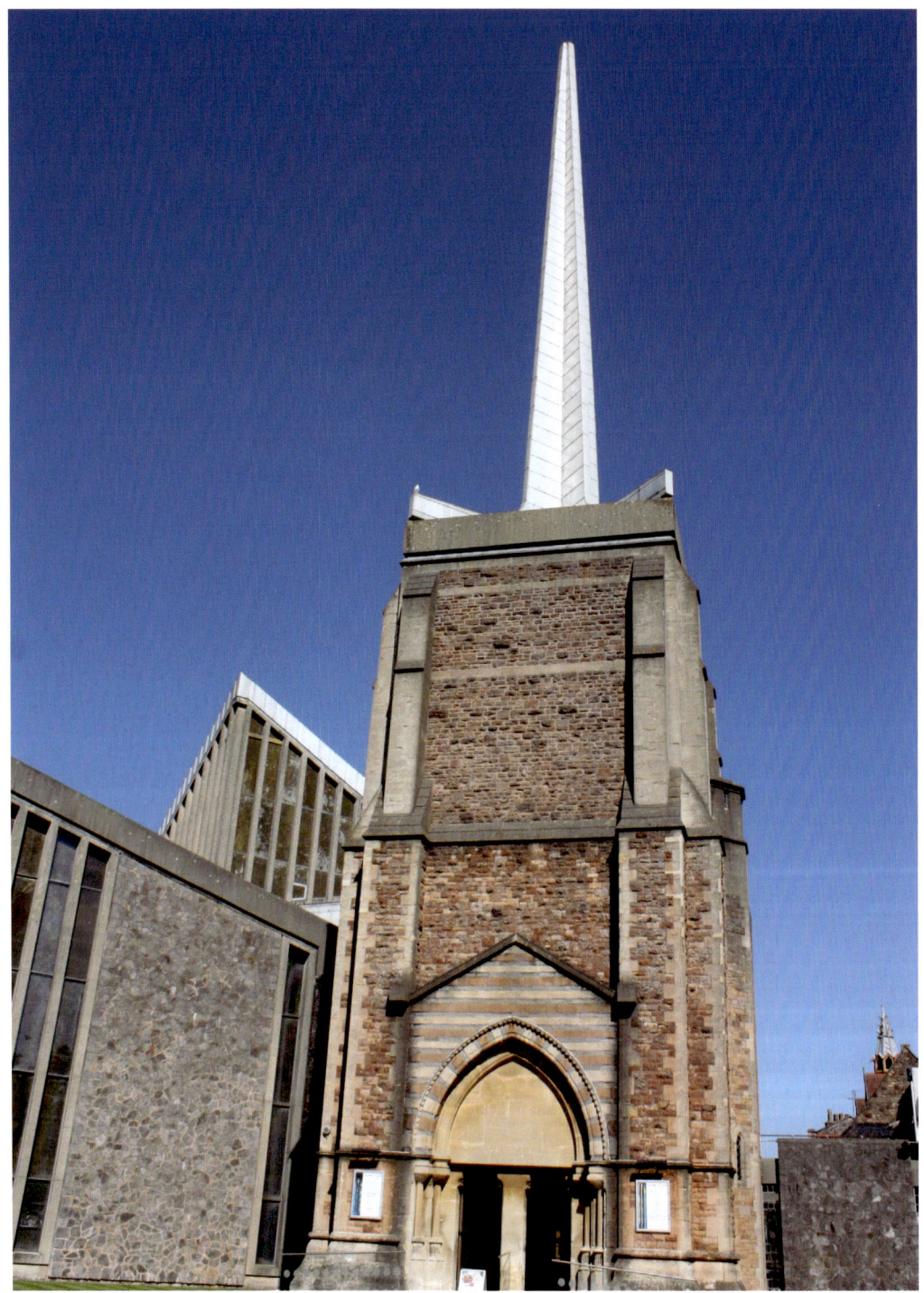

All Saints' Church, Clifton, with unusual aluminium-clad spire. (Courtesy of Trevor Naylor)

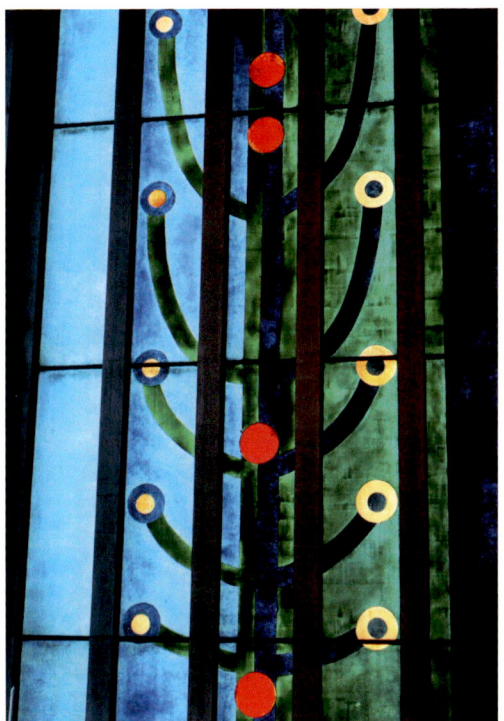 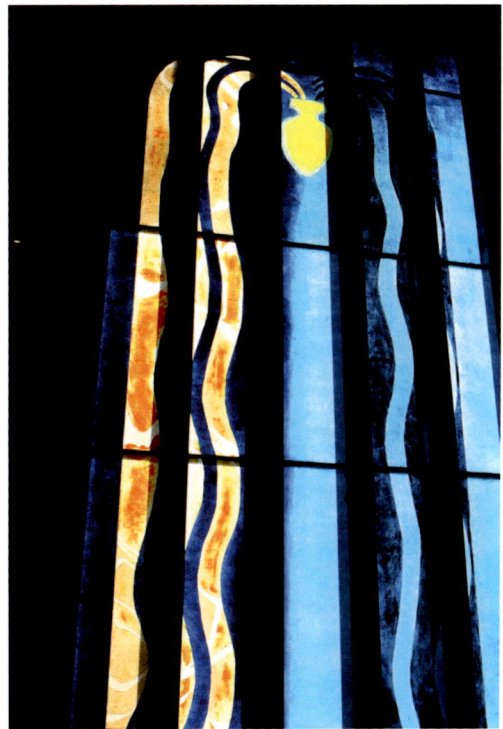

Above left, above right and below: John Piper windows in All Saints' Church, Clifton. (Courtesy of Trevor Naylor)

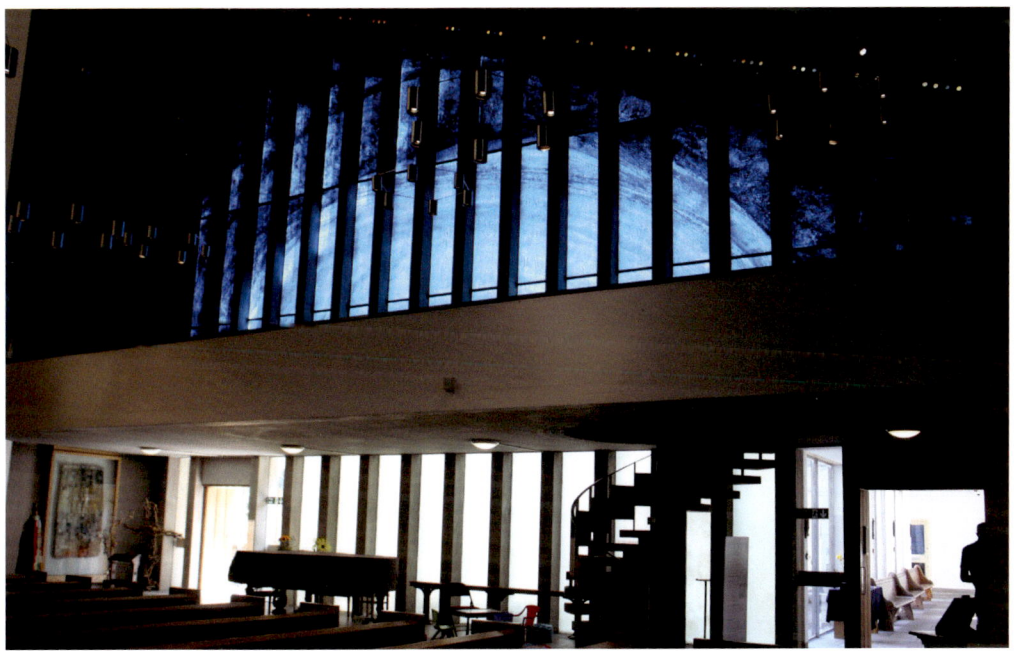

During the Second World War, All Saints' was totally destroyed when it was burnt out by incendiary bombs in a night-time air raid in December 1940. Despite brave efforts by neighbours and boys from the nearby Clifton College to save the church, bombs from the German Luftwaffe quickly destroyed the fabric of the chancel and the roof of the nave. Masonry was also extensively damaged.

For the next two decades or so arguments raged over whether All Saints' should be rebuilt or the site used for a garden of remembrance. The diocese of Bristol favoured demolition of the ruins and asking the congregation to worship at Emmanuel Church nearby. There was strong opposition from both congregations and eventually it was decided that All Saints' Church should be rebuilt.

The church authorities wanted the design to be ultra-modern and to incorporate the base of the original tower, which had been left standing. A landmark feature of the rebuilt church is its 138-foot-high aluminium-clad laminated timber spire. The largest mobile crane in Europe at the time (1967) was needed to lift the spire into position. It cost £4,000 and that was without the bill for putting the spire into place. All Saints' Church was ready for its first service on 1 July 1967.

Visitors in the nave can be forgiven for thinking they are standing in an art gallery for they are surrounded by windows formed from fibreglass and polyester on to which the artist John Piper (1903–92) poured coloured resins. The first impression inside the church is of light and colour. Piper's interpretation of the Bible's Book of Revelation has a stunning effect, with its vibrant colours of red, green, yellow and blue all standing out. All Saints', Clifton, was the first church where John Piper operated through the medium of fibre glass. It was strikingly modern at the time of its creation and has been hugely admired ever since. Other windows at All Saints' feature the colour blue, which Piper used in his vision of the Creation.

Piper's link with All Saints' Church is not the only artistic connection he had with Bristol. In the early years of the Second World War, Piper was appointed as an official War Artist. This meant that he was in Bristol shortly after the first big night-time air raid in the city in November 1940. Among the ruins he sketched was St Mary Le Port Church, on the edge of what is now Castle Green and Temple Church, near Temple Meads railway station.

12. Emmanuel Church, Clifton

The 110-foot-high tower of Emmanuel Church is still a significant landmark in Clifton, although the rest of the church has been demolished and residential accommodation built in its place.

The church was built of stone that had been quarried nearby. Construction of the church and the land it stood on cost a total of £3,500. This amount was largely raised through private subscriptions, although there was a grant of £200 from the Bristol-based Society of Merchant Venturers.

When the church was consecrated in 1869 it had room for 614 worshippers. It was built to offer people living nearby a different style of worship from the Anglo-Catholic liturgy used at All Saints' Church around the corner in Pembroke Road. The services there follow the Church of England faith but incorporate Catholic

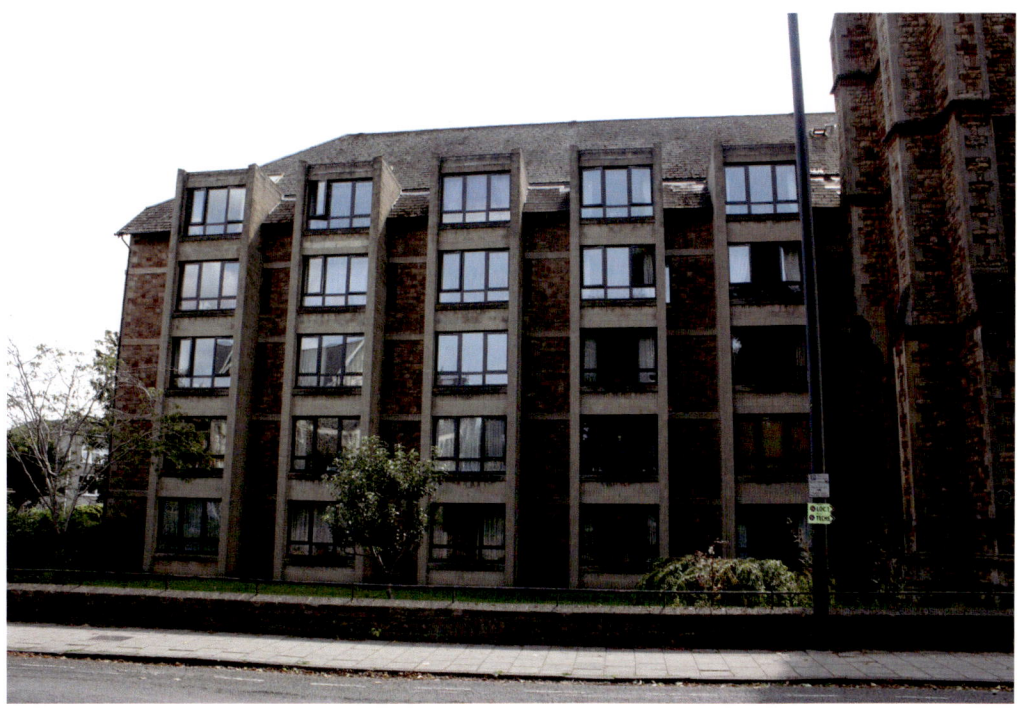

Site of Emmanuel Church, now converted into apartments. (Courtesy of Trevor Naylor)

traditions. This was regarded as 'High Church' while Emmanuel was considered to be 'Low Church' and more of the evangelic wing.

Emmanuel Church survived fire bombing in the Second World War, but fell into the mouth of the bulldozer after the diocese of Bristol declared it redundant in the late 1960s. Its tower was kept and incorporated into Emmanuel Court, a £600,000 block of flats for elderly people. The flats, which stand on the site of Emmanuel Church, were officially opened in 1982 by the Duchess of Kent.

The church has had a touch of literary fame too. On Christmas Eve in 1914 the vicar found time to squeeze in a wedding ceremony at short notice between the festive services. It had been organised rather hastily the day before when the bride and groom obtained a special licence from the bishop. The groom was on leave from the Royal Air Force at the time. On the couple's wedding certificate, the bride is described as a spinster and the bridegroom as a captain in the Royal Flying Corps. The bride was twenty-four-year old Agatha Miller from Torquay and the groom was Archibald Christie, whose address was given as Guthrie Road, Clifton, where his stepfather, who was a master at neighbouring Clifton College, lived. The church was in the same road. Using her married name of Agatha Christie, the bride went on to write more than seventy detective novels featuring the Belgian detective Hercule Poirot and the village spinster Miss Jane Marple. The Christies' marriage lasted fourteen years, ending in a divorce in 1928.

13. CHRIST CHURCH, CLIFTON

Three different architects working at three different times designed various sections of the magnificent Christ Church, a Grade II* listed building. It stands in a prominent position on the edge of Clifton and Durdham Downs (440 acres of wooded and open grassland in the north-west corner of Bristol).

The body of the church was built in 1841 in an Early English Gothic Revival architectural style by Charles Dyer, the son of a Bristol surgeon. The steeple of Christ Church was added by John Norton in 1859, an architect known for designing churches and country houses. London architect William Bassett-Smith built the aisles in 1885. It was consecrated in 1844, although it was far from complete. The church was built at a time when prosperous merchants, many of them involved in the shipping trade, were moving into Clifton away from the hustle and bustle of the town and its harbour.

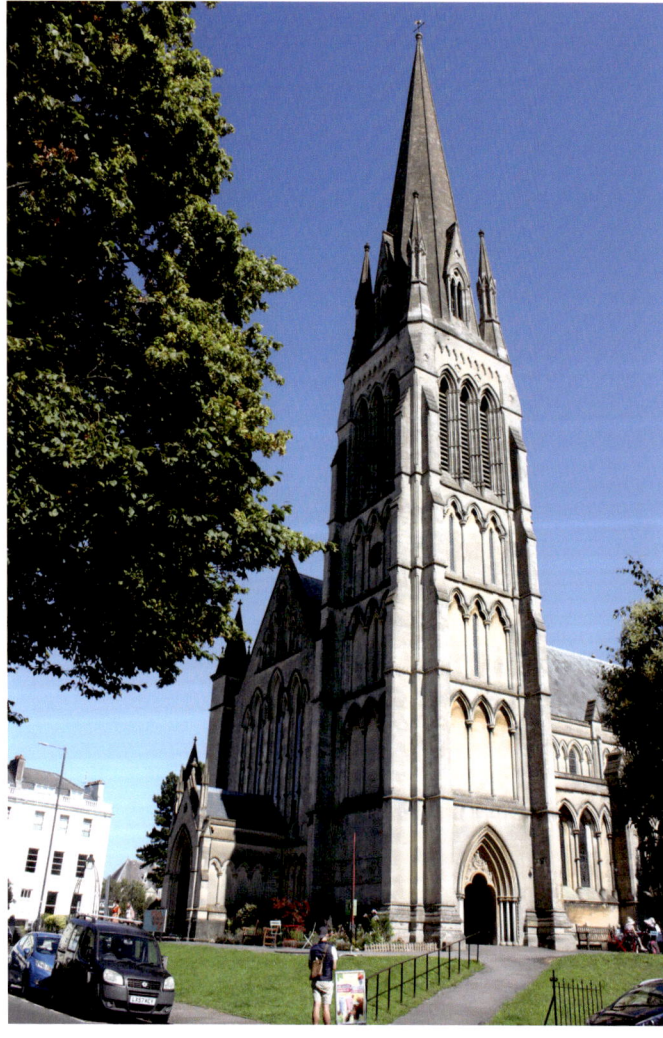

Christ Church, Clifton, showing its impressive tall spire. (Courtesy of Trevor Naylor)

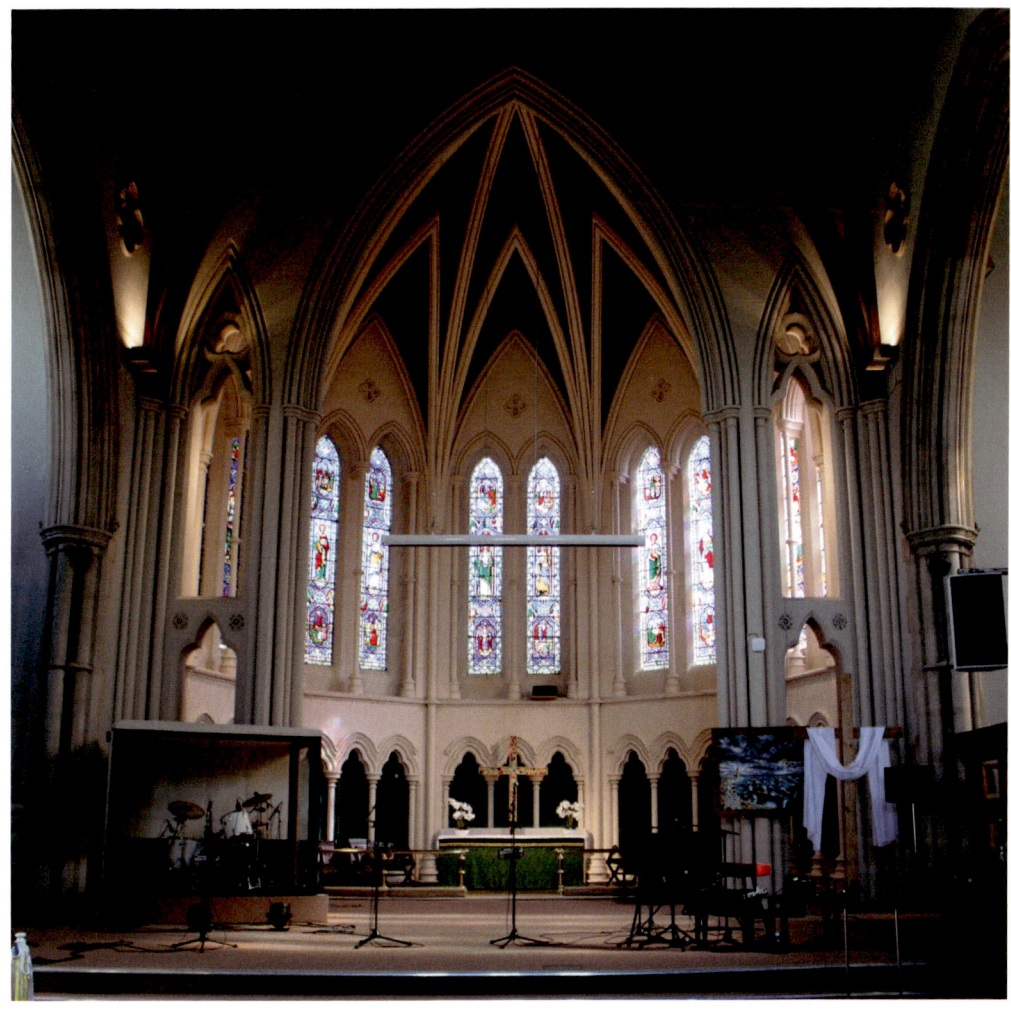

Interior view of Christ Church, Clifton. (Courtesy of Trevor Naylor)

To help meet the cost of building the church – £10,000 – and buying the land – another £500 – a church rate, a local form of taxation, was introduced. When building work was finished the church had room for more than 1,000 worshippers. It is said that when the spire of Christ Church was completed, one of the workmen was so delighted that he did a headstand on the quarter-ton capstone at 212 feet above street level.

In the winter of 1872, a storm brought one of the pinnacles crashing down on the organ and through the gallery into the floor below. Fortunately, no one was hurt. As a precaution against further similar incidents, the remaining pinnacles were strengthened. In 2015 the church was closed for two weeks after the steeple was damaged in high winds.

A former curate at Christ Church was later appointed Bishop of Liverpool. The Rt Revd James Jones was bishop from 1998 to 2013. He was appointed Knight Commander of the British Empire (KBE) in the 2017 New Year Honours List, recognising his services to bereaved families and justice.

Christ Church was originally the daughter church of nearby St Andrew's, but became the parish church itself after St Andrew's was bombed in the Second World War and the ruins later demolished. The church has never been replaced.

A replica of Christ Church has been built in Thames Town, a suburb of Shanghai in China. It is built in a style that is imitative of English architecture.

14. St Nicholas' Church, Baldwin Street

This is believed to be the third church by the name of St Nicholas to have stood on the same site. Interestingly, the medieval crypt, which formed part of the old city wall, remains to this day. When the church was taken down and rebuilt in 1769 the nave and tower were rebuilt in Georgian Gothic Revival style. This Grade II* listed church is prominently sited opposite historic Bristol Bridge, the first crossing over the River Avon that flows through the centre of Bristol. The church is built on a steeply sloping site between St Nicholas Street and Baldwin Street. Above its tower is a spire that rises 205 feet and is a landmark across the centre of the city. The clock on the tower is believed to be the only church clock in the country with a seconds hand. The clockwork was destroyed during the Blitz but was later repaired and converted to electricity so that it still works today.

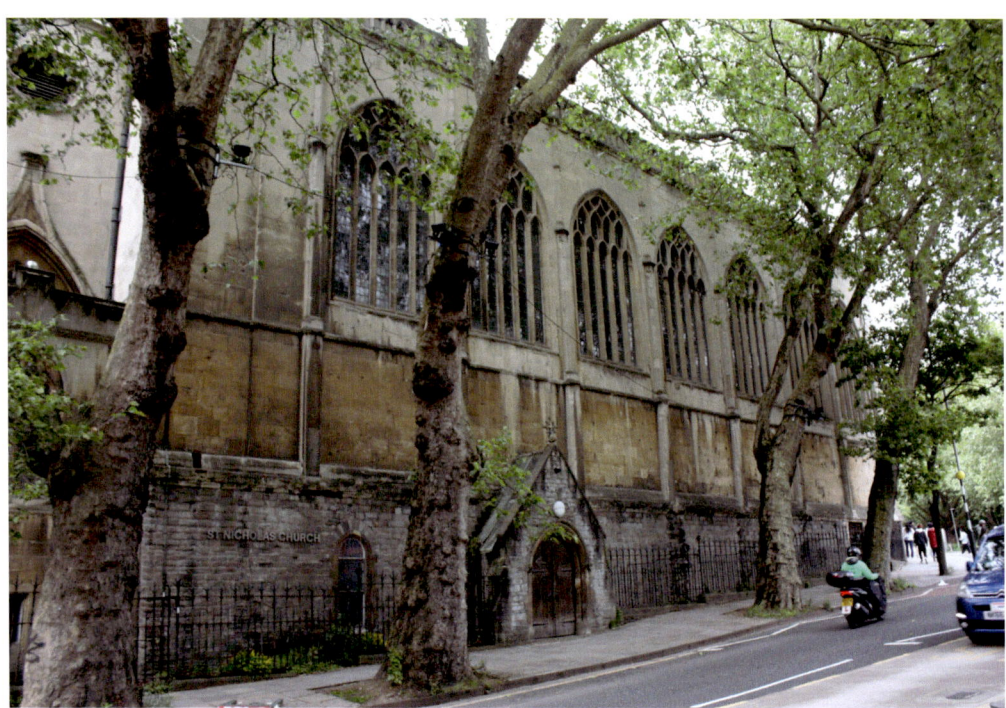

St Nicholas' Church. (Courtesy of Trevor Naylor)

Church records state that a curfew bell was rung daily at 9 p.m. to inform all good citizens it was time to damp down their fires at home and retire to bed. In 1481 the church sacristan received instructions to ring the curfew for fifteen minutes each night or face a fine of 2*d*.

The original church is believed to have been founded in the eleventh century, with its chancel built upon the town wall over St Nicholas Gate. A brass plaque found in the crypt in 1823 gives the year 1030 as the date of the church's foundation.

An outstanding feature of the old chancel was the dozen steps of alternate black and white marble that worshippers had to ascend to reach the altar.

In days of old, St Nicholas' Church maintained with great ceremony the unusual festival of the Boy Bishop. This tradition was held on the feast day of St Nicholas, the patron saint of children, and involved one of the choirboys being selected to act as bishop for the day. With the exception of saying Mass, the Boy Bishop, wearing a richly coloured episcopal robe and mitre and carrying a crozier, would conduct all the services for the day. The occasion was treated with such seriousness that the mayor of Bristol and their civic colleagues, along with the sheriff of Bristol, attended evening service to hear the Boy Bishop's sermon and receive his blessing.

A remarkable feat occurred at St Nicholas' Church in October 1816 when a marble mason undertook to repair the weathervane. Finding his ladder too short to reach the iron cross at the top of the steeple, he made a leap and caught hold of the iron on which the weathervane was fastened. He then seated himself astride and took off the weathervane, which weighed 33 pounds; before descending with it, he waved it over his head two or three times.

One of the monuments in the church is that of Alderman John Whitson, a philanthropist and founder of Red Maids High School. He was a parishioner of St Nicholas' and was buried in the crypt, where his three wives and one daughter also lie at rest. Whitson is especially remembered each November when girls of Red Maids visit St Nicholas' Church to lay a wreath on his tomb. Afterwards, the students process through the centre of the city in their red robes and white bonnets to Bristol Cathedral for a special service marking the school's Founder's Day.

On the night of 24 November 1940, the interior of St Nicholas' Church was destroyed by bombing in the first major air raid the city experienced in the Second World War. Bombing destroyed the eighteenth-century rococo interior. The church was restored in 1975 as an ecclesiastical museum. The museum closed in 2007 and the building was used by the city council as offices. In 2018, St Nicholas' Church came back into use as an Anglican church, with the first service for sixty years being held just before Christmas.

The building we see today is of a Georgian Gothic style. It was redesigned by James Bridges, an American architect who worked in Bristol from 1756 to 1763. The crypt has its own entrance in Baldwin Street, while the main church is entered at a higher level in St Nicholas Street.

It was this church that the Bristol-born Poet Laureate Robert Southey once described 'a modern church and spire, so beautifully proportioned, and therefore so fine, that you do not at first perceive that the whole building is perfectly plain and unornamented'.

15. THE CATHEDRAL CHURCH OF ST PETER AND ST PAUL, CLIFTON

When Cardinal Heenan, Archbishop of Westminster, consecrated the Cathedral Church of St Peter and St Paul, popularly known as Clifton Cathedral, he told the congregation: 'This is the ecclesiastical bargain of the century.' The cardinal pointed out in his sermon that most of the cost of £600,000 was met by 'the generosity of a few benefactors'.

The cathedral was completed in just over three years, which, according to the building industry, was the fastest such project undertaken in Britain since the Middle Ages. The Concrete Society named it as 'the best concrete building completed in England in 1973'.

When the cathedral was completed, the architects were awarded the Bronze Medal of the Royal Institution of British Architects.

The cathedral was consecrated during a service lasting two hours. The Order of Service included much pomp and pageantry with various processions, which included not only Roman Catholic clergy but also Church of England bishops, civic leaders from various parts of the West Country and Members of Parliament.

The architects designed the cathedral with the decisions of the Second Vatican Council in mind. The interior is therefore flexible and affords a space where a congregation of almost a thousand people can easily feel themselves closely involved with the celebration of Mass. The architects chose reinforced concrete to construct the cathedral because it reduced external noise and assisted thermal storage. Clad in large panels of Aberdeen granite of a pinkish-brown colour, it was designed to blend in with the Bath stone and Brandon stone that had been used in the construction of surrounding homes. The building is crowned by three concrete spires rising 167 feet from the top of a lantern tower. They are part of the ultra-modern design of this hexagonal building which contrasts with the neighbouring Georgian houses in this densely built part of Clifton.

Thanks to the design of the cathedral, 1,000 worshippers are able to see the high altar without any pillars or other obstructions standing in their way. Indeed, no one is sat more than 50 feet away from the altar. Most of the cathedral's interior furnishings are contemporary.

The cathedral is the seat of the Roman Catholic Bishop of Clifton and the 'mother church' of Roman Catholics not only in Bristol but also in the adjoining counties of Somerset, Gloucestershire and Wiltshire.

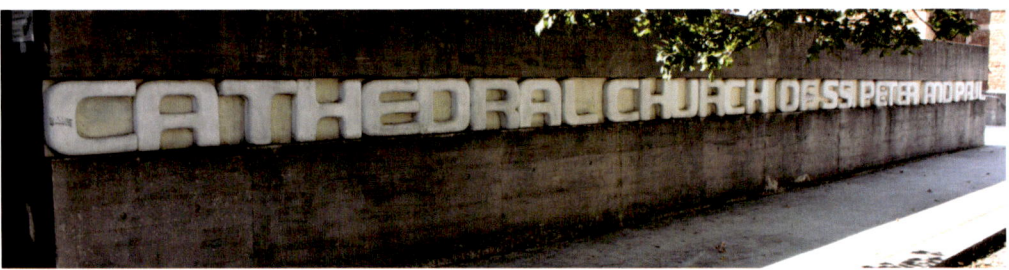

Clifton Cathedral, a modern concrete structure. (Courtesy of Trevor Naylor)

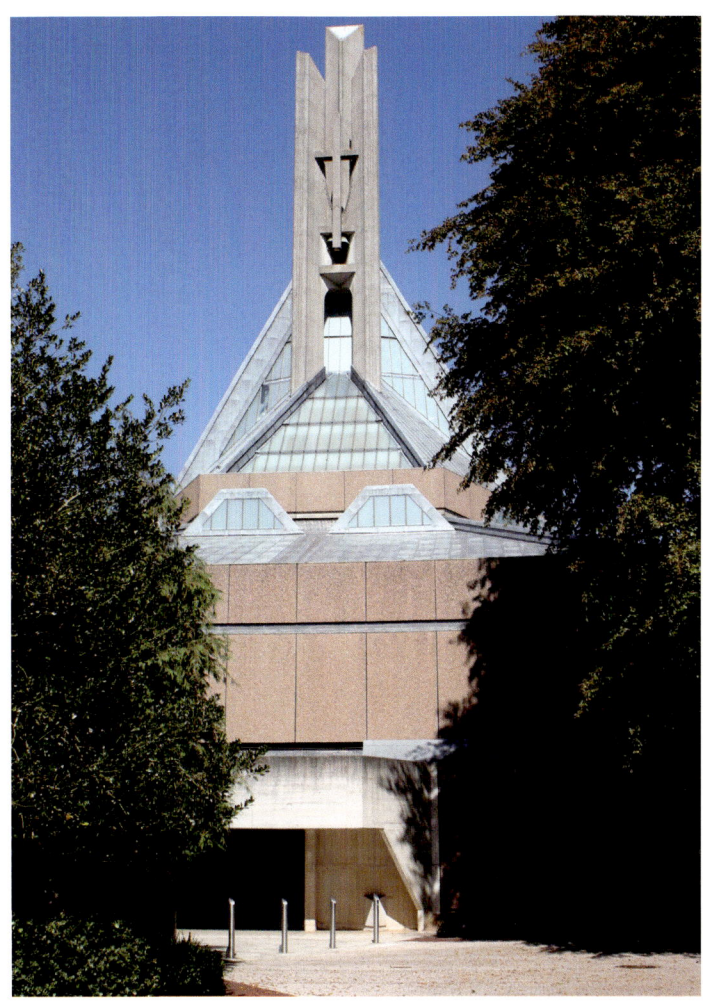

The entrance to Clifton Cathedral. (Courtesy of Trevor Naylor)

This modern cathedral replaces the Church of the Holy Apostles in Park Place, also in Clifton. When Pope Pius IX created the diocese of Clifton in 1850 the church was designated a pro-cathedral, a title to be used until a cathedral could be built. In the 1960s major work costing up to £100,000 was needed at the pro-cathedral to make it generally stable. However, the architects and builders could not guarantee that after the work was carried out, more would not be needed in twenty years' time.

The pro-cathedral was built on a steeply sloping 15-acre site. It was described as an architectural melange of the classic and Gothic building styles. After it was deconsecrated the pro-cathedral's fixtures and furnishings were put up for auction. Among the many lots that went under the auctioneer's hammer were stained-glass windows, a Victorian pulpit, confessional boxes and statues. Some of the bids came via telephone from overseas buyers. The pro-cathedral has since been converted into residential accommodation.

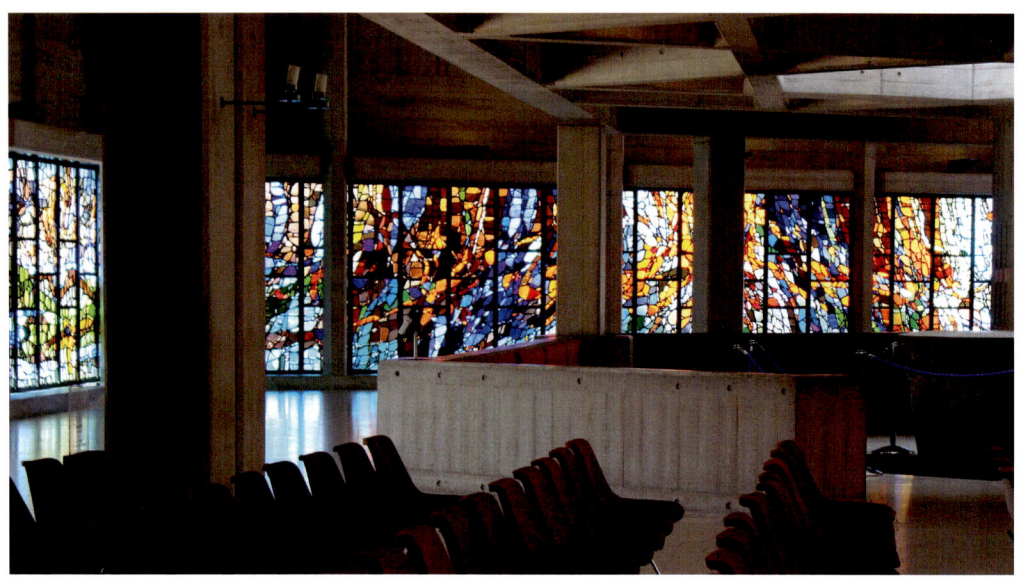

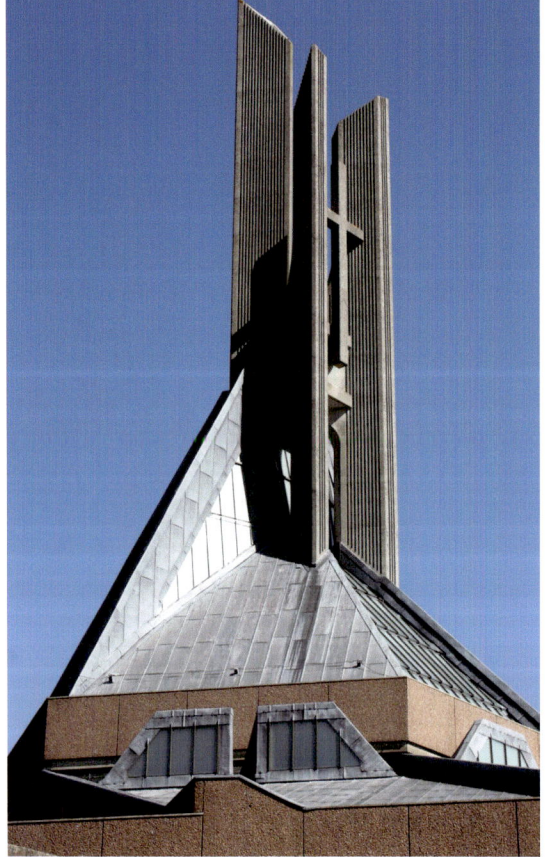

Above: Clifton Cathedral's impressive stained-glass windows. (Courtesy of Trevor Naylor)

Left: The three spires of Clifton Cathedral. (Courtesy of Trevor Naylor)

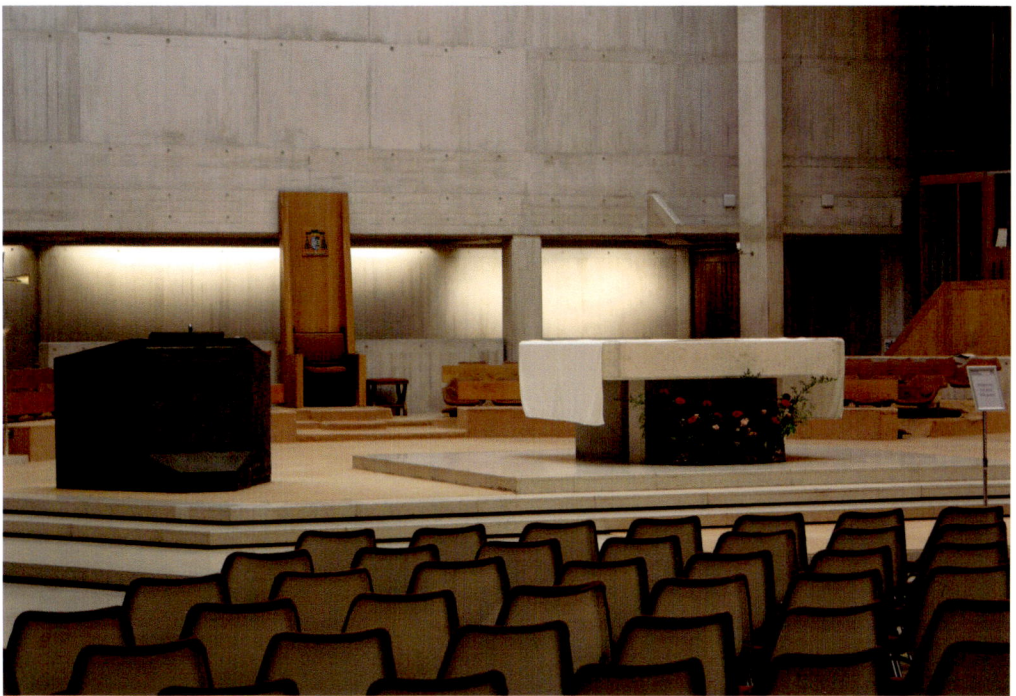

Interior view of Clifton Cathedral. (Courtesy of Trevor Naylor)

16. St Paul's Church, Southville

The first St Paul's Church in south Bristol was consecrated on 24 October 1831 during the famous Bristol riots, when it is said that several thousand people were present. A local newspaper reported that it was such an important occasion for a new church to come into use that all the ships in the harbour displayed their flags and sounded their horns. Twenty-one guns were also fired in what is known as a royal salute. The newspaper stated that 'ruffians attacked the carriage of the Bishop of Bath & Wells as he was leaving the church'. The protests were against the bishop voting against the Reform Bill, which was then being debated in Parliament.

During the next 100 years or so, the congregation at St Paul's Church grew into one of the largest in Bristol. However, disaster struck the building shortly before midnight on 11 April 1941 (Good Friday) when it was destroyed in a Second World War air raid. All that was left standing were the four walls of the church and the tower. Everything else was reduced to burning ashes. It was one of the worst air raids on Bristol, with St Paul's receiving a direct hit from Luftwaffe bombs. Remarkably, 300 people who had sought refuge in the crypt escaped unscathed, which some people described as a modern-day miracle.

Ten brides due to walk down the aisle of St Paul's the next day on Easter Saturday found that their weddings had been transferred to the nearby daughter church of

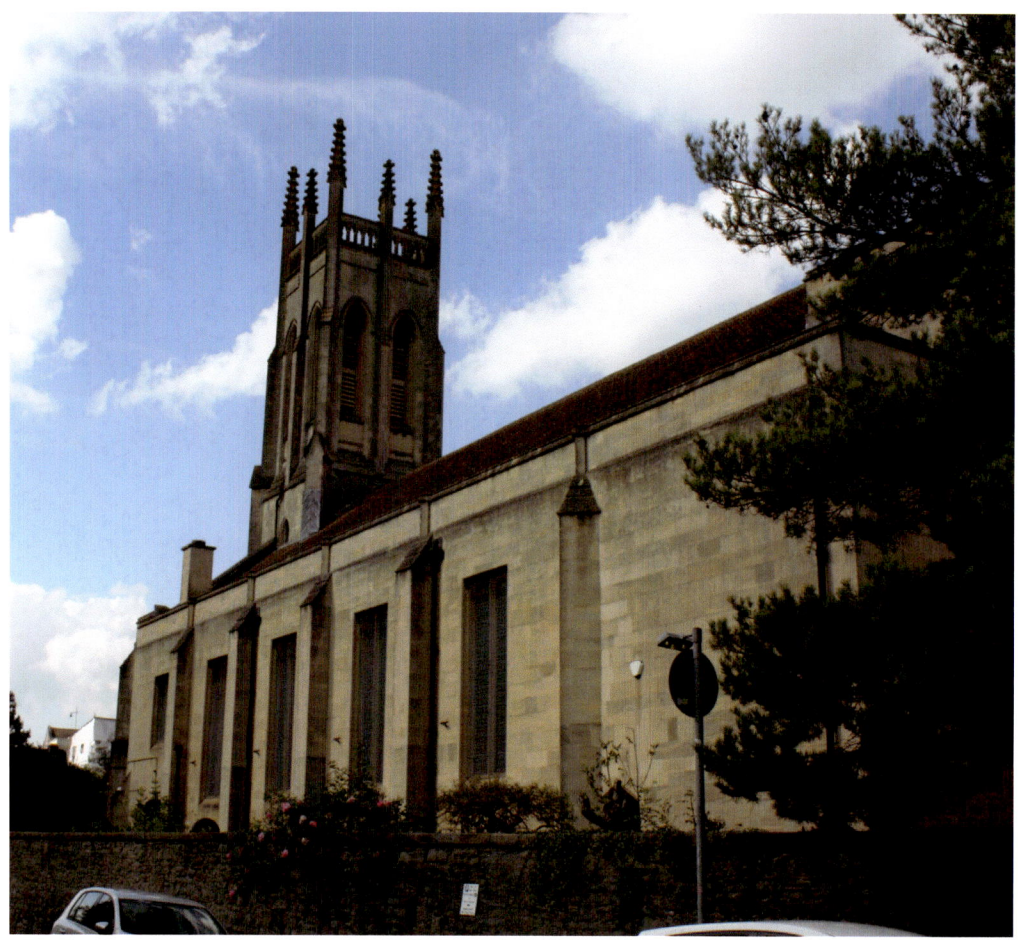

St Paul's Church, Southville. (Courtesy of Trevor Naylor)

St David's. This became the temporary parish church until 22 March 1958, when rebuilding work on St Paul's Church was complete and services could be held there once again.

St Paul's Church was originally built after the Church Commissioners received an application from people living in the Southville area requesting that a new church be built to accommodate the growing number of people arriving to live in the area. Seven years later land that formed part of a plot known as 'Three Acres Ground' was bought by the church authorities for £600 on the condition that it was used for ecclesiastical purposes only.

Disaster hit the church again in 1990 when strong winds brought 40 tonnes of masonry crashing through the roof, wrecking the balcony, damaging pews and other furniture. Damage cost £250,000 and took two years to repair. Ironically, the disaster happened on the feast day of St Paul. A year later to the day, the then Bishop of Bristol, the Rt Revd Barry Rogerson, swapped his mitre for a workman's hard hat to conduct a service of Holy Communion amid the ruins of the church. He offered prayers of blessing on the repair work that was in progress. Afterwards he told reporters: 'Things like the destruction of a church do bring people closer together and that is what has happened here.' He admitted that he had never conducted a church service quite like it before. While restoration work was going ahead, services at St Paul's Church were switched to St David's Hall once again.

The national spotlight fell on St Paul's Church on 13 March 1994 when the BBC broadcast a Eucharist celebrated by the vicar, Revd Val Woods. She had been ordained into the Church of England priesthood the previous day at Bristol Cathedral – less than a mile away as the proverbial crow flies south – and this was the first televised Church of England Eucharist celebrated by a woman.

17. St Mary on the Quay, Colston Avenue

St Mary on the Quay must have once been a picture-postcard scene: ships moored right in front of the church with its imposing portico of six Greek Corinthian columns. Tethering rings were built into the front wall of the church so that ships could be safely tied to the building while they were docked in Bristol's harbour. In 1893 the harbour was covered over and this has become one of Bristol's busiest roads, with cars, coaches, lorries vans and buses trundling past St Mary's at all hours of the day. The tethering rings have long been removed from the church wall.

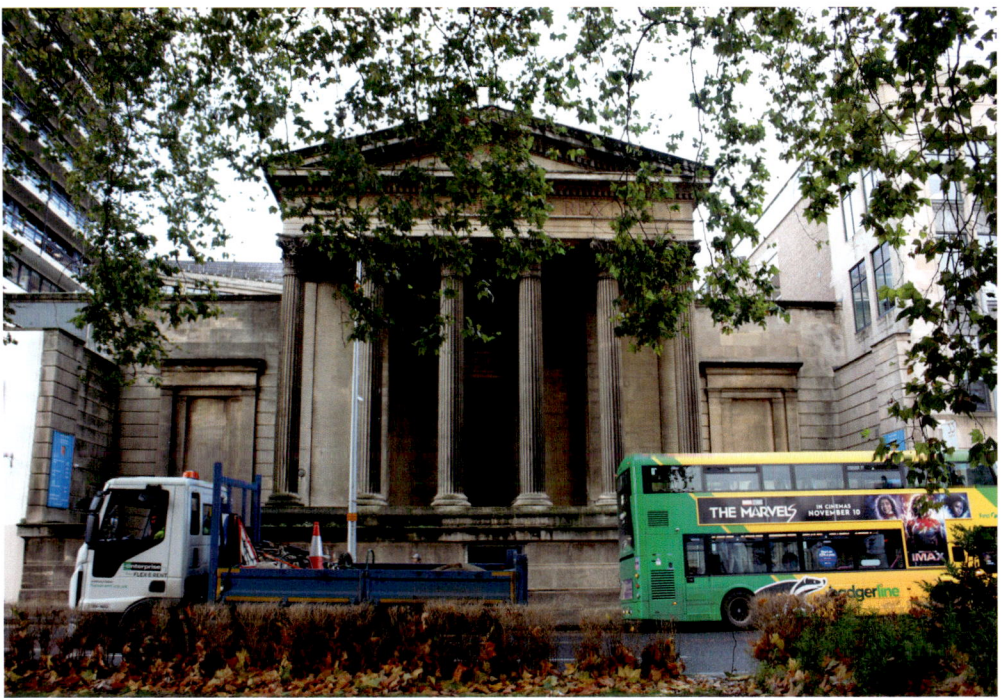

St Mary on the Quay, once on the harbour side. (Courtesy of Trevor Naylor)

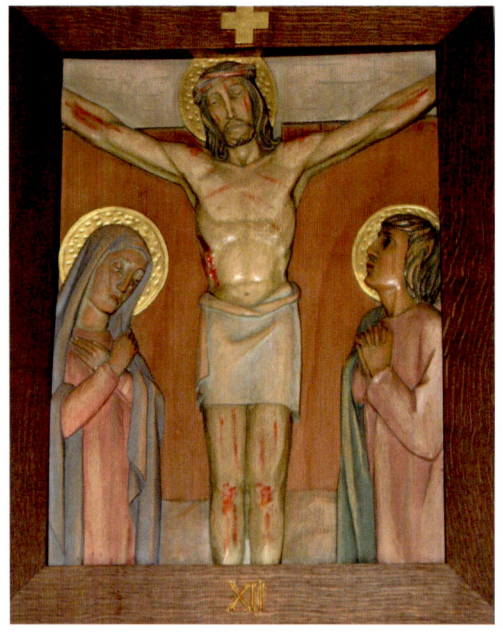
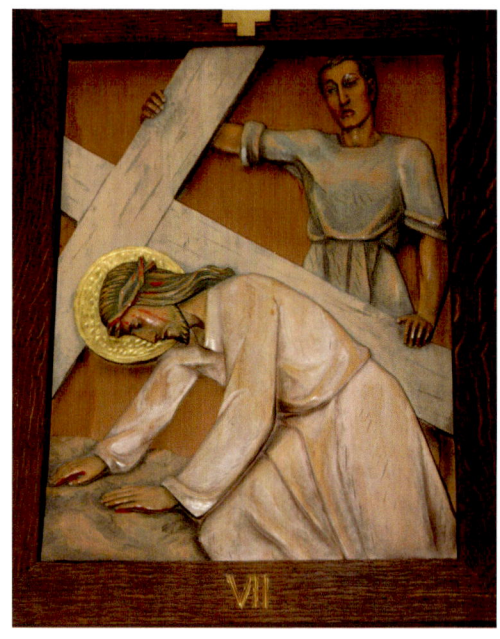

Above left and above right: St Mary on the Quay, Stations of the Cross. (Courtesy of Trevor Naylor)

Left: Interior view of St Mary on the Quay. (Courtesy of Trevor Naylor)

St Mary's was originally built for the Catholic Apostolic Church, also known as the Irvingites, an evangelical sect, in 1840. However, three years later the Irvingites, who had financial problems and dwindling congregations, sold the building to the Roman Catholic Church.

This Grade II* listed building, designated as such for both architectural and historical reasons, is the oldest Roman Catholic church in the city. Its interior is rectangular and mainly plain, save for Corinthian columns at the entrance to the Sanctuary.

The *Bristol Mercury*, a weekly newspaper, wrote: 'The erection, is considered by competent judges to be one of the purest specimens of Greek architecture in the kingdom and is certainly ranked among the most beautiful edifices in the city.'

St Mary on the Quay, which has room for 600 people at its services, is administered by the Roman Catholic diocese of Clifton.

18. St Mark's Chapel (The Lord Mayor's Chapel), College Green

On the north side of College Green, rubbing shoulders with a row of twentieth-century shops and immediately facing Bristol Cathedral, is a unique place of worship which was founded more than 800 years ago. It is the only church or chapel in England that is owned by a local authority (or perhaps it would be more correct to say that it is owned by Bristol City Council's taxpayers!). It is also unusual in that the chapel does not have a parish or its own.

The church is formally dedicated to St Mark but is more affectionately known by the people of Bristol as the Lord Mayor's Chapel. It is the only remaining building of the Hospital of St Mark, which was founded in around 1230 and was connected to St Augustine's Abbey, known today as Bristol Cathedral. The hospital provided food and care for 100 people every day. The church's red sandstone tower, completed in 1487, is best viewed from College Green.

Wealthy merchants of Bristol endowed St Mark's with various manors and lands in Gloucestershire, Somerset and Wiltshire, as well as the land immediately surrounding the chapel including the nearby Orchard Street, which was the site of St Mark's Orchard.

Much of the chapel was built in the Early English architectural style. It has been regularly updated and refurbished. Along with the St Augustine's Abbey, it was closed in 1539 when Henry VIII broke away from the Roman Catholic Church to form the Church of England.

In 1541 the organisation that became Bristol City Council bought the chapel and its lands for £1,000. Later, the mayor and Bristol Corporation offered French Huguenots use of the chapel after they had fled their homeland. In 1722 it was fitted up to become the official place of worship of the mayor of Bristol, councillors and aldermen, and has remained so ever since. Before this council officials attended divine service at Bristol Cathedral. However, after a dispute with the dean and chapter they decided to use St Mark's Chapel.

Traditionally, High Court judges, robed in red and bewigged, arrived by horse-drawn carriage for a special service with the lord mayor at St Mark's Chapel before going on to dispense justice at a new session of the Bristol Assize Courts. This was always a colourful and historic event; however, it fell by the wayside with the introduction of the Crown Court in 1974 and the abolition of the assizes.

The chapel has some interior fixtures not usually seen in a church. The whole of the floor of the Jesus Chapel is laid with sixteenth-century Spanish tiles, intermixed with a few Early English tiles. This is believed to be the largest floor area of Spanish tiles of this date outside Spain. Near the lord mayor's seat is the stand (or rest) for Bristol's state sword. Brass brackets on each side of another stand hold the silver mace, which police officers carry as they process in front of the lord mayor on State visits. There is also a special place where the City Sword Bearer can place their Cap of Maintenance during a service.

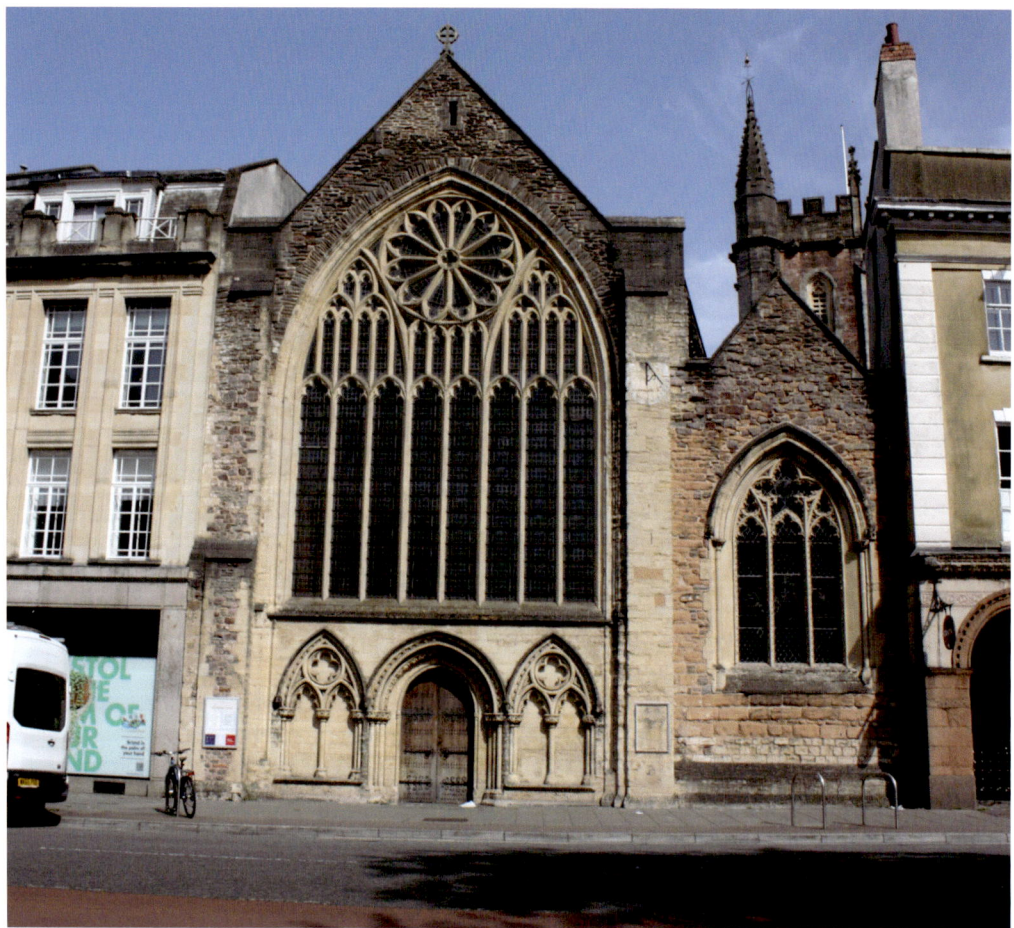

Lord Mayor's Chapel surrounded by commercial buildings. (Courtesy of Trevor Naylor)

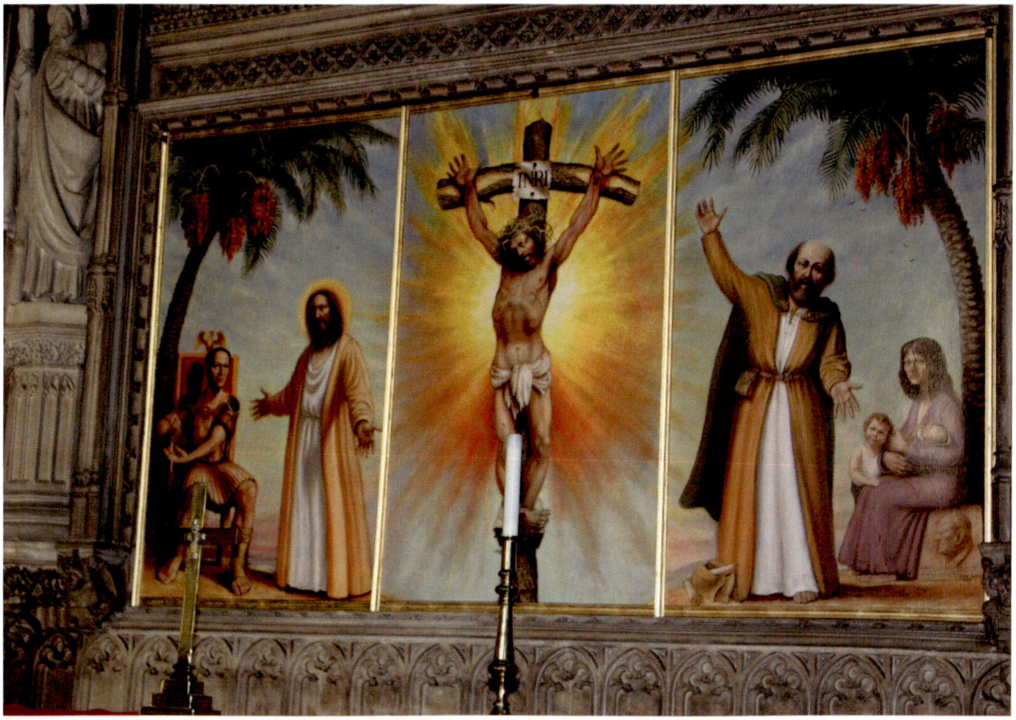

Above: Lord Mayor's Chapel contains many impressive pieces of art. (Courtesy of Trevor Naylor)

Below: Lord Mayor's Chapel seating. (Courtesy of Trevor Naylor)

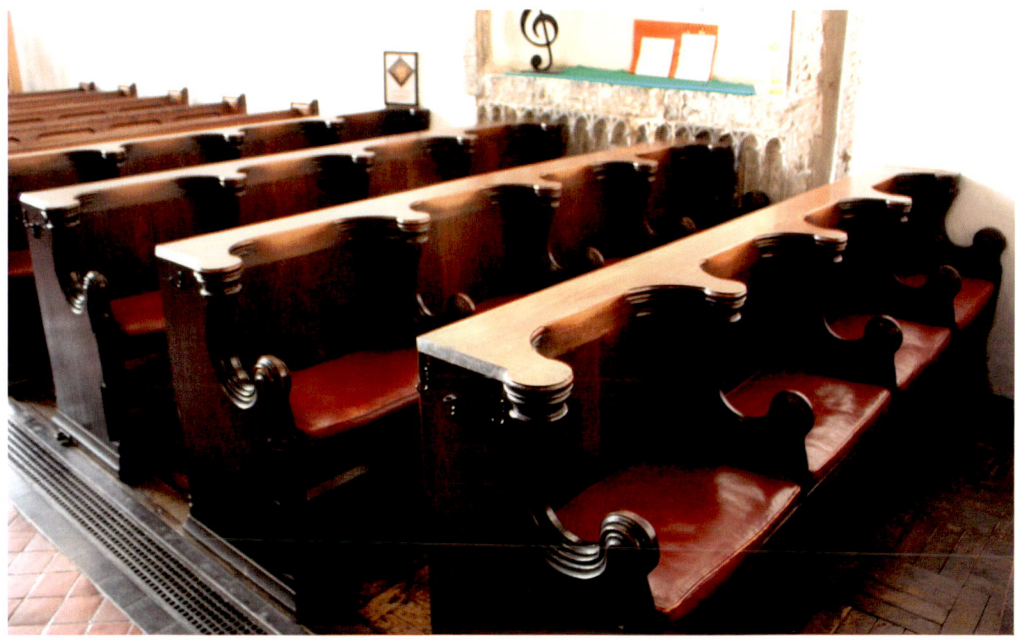

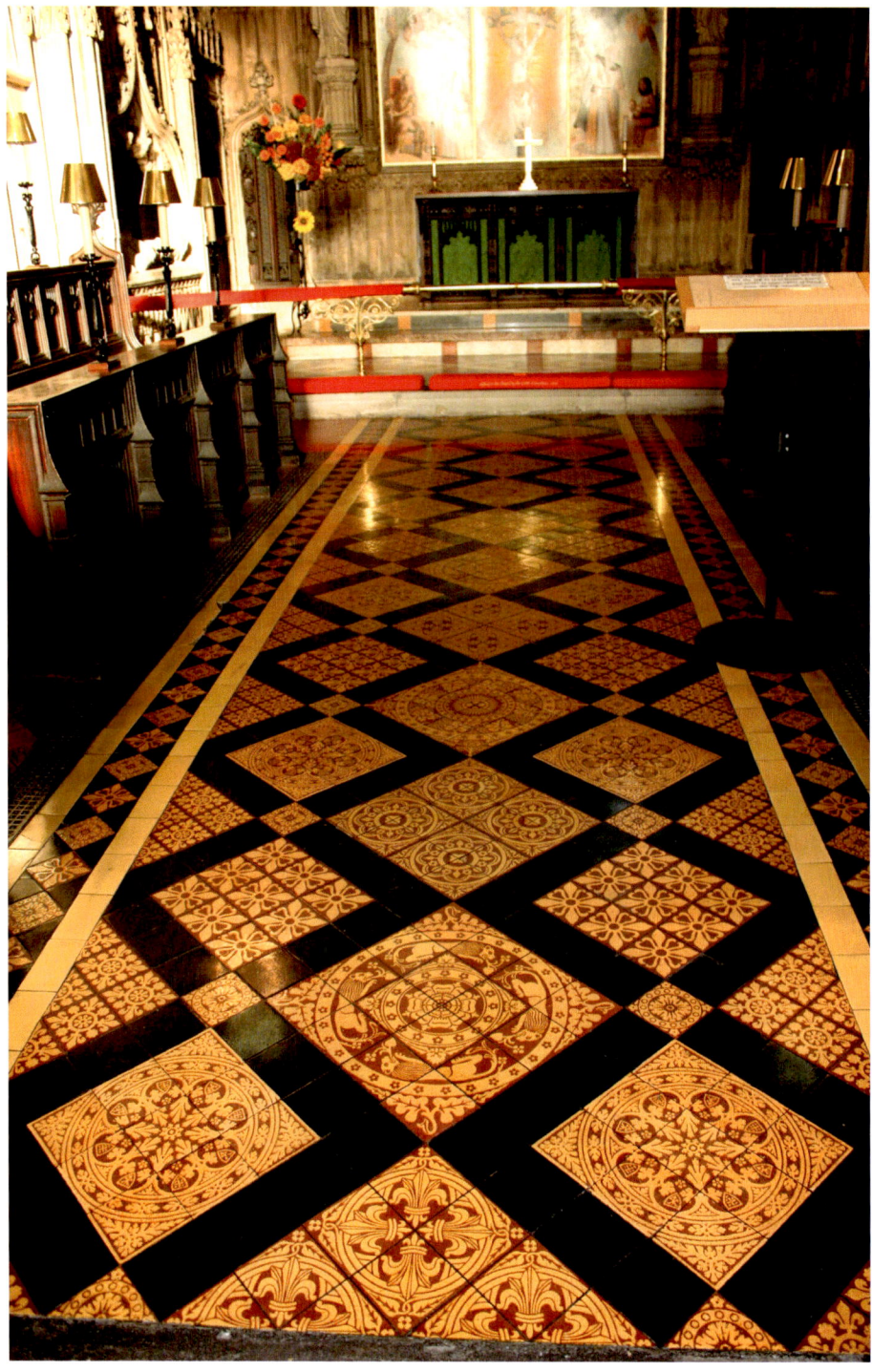

Ornate floor tiles, Lord Mayor's Chapel. (Courtesy of Trevor Naylor)

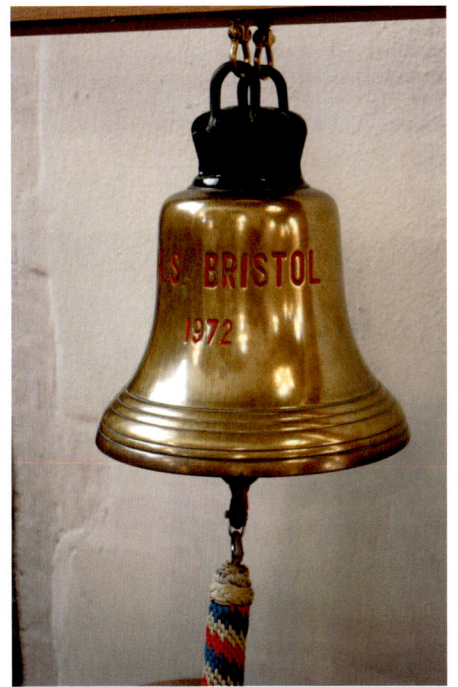 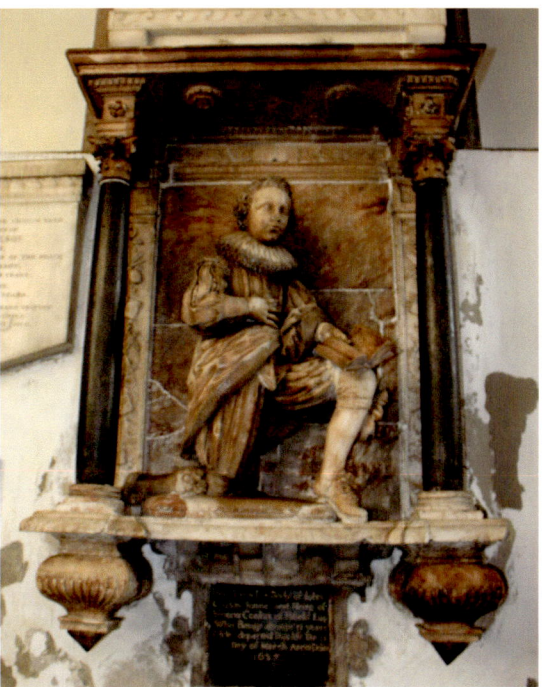

Above left: Ship's bell from HMS *Bristol*, Lord Mayor's Chapel. (Courtesy of Trevor Naylor)

Above right: Tomb of John Cookin, Lord Mayor's Chapel. (Courtesy of Trevor Naylor)

The church is built on a north–south line rather than the usual east–west alignment. It contains effigies of the church's founders in chain mail, medieval tombs and post-Reformation monuments, as well as ironwork brought from the bombed Temple Church made by the Bristol craftsman William Edney. His gates separate the south aisle from the south aisle chapel.

In the eighteenth century one of the preachers at the Lord Mayor's Chapel was John Wesley, founder of Methodism. The bishop had banned John Wesley from preaching in Bristol churches, so the mayor invited him to preach in what was effectively his own chapel.

The chapel holds a memorial sculpted in alabaster to John Cookin. Little is known about him, except that he died in 1627 at the age of eleven years.

Since 2023 the Lord Mayor's Chapel has been cared for (on behalf of the city council) by Bristol Cathedral. Services, which are open to everyone, are held there every Sunday.

19. The Church of St George, Brandon Hill

One of the first grants made under the Government's Church Building Act of 1818 went to the Church of St George, which was built on a steep slope between Great George Street and Charlotte Street off the top of Park Street, close to the centre of Bristol. It became the first building in the city to be constructed in the Greek Revival style.

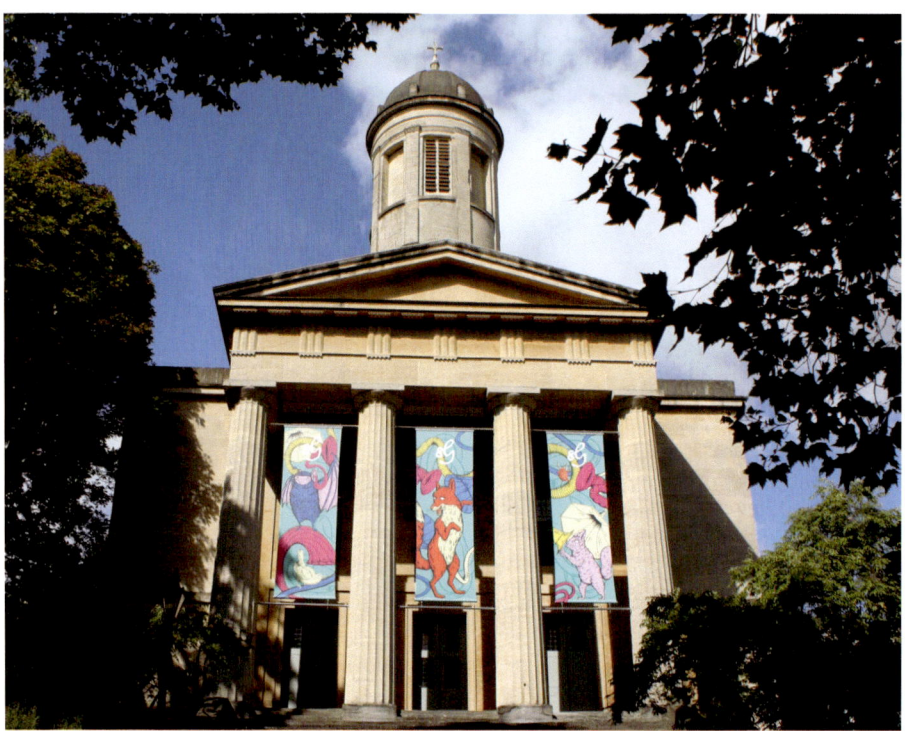

Above: St George's, now an international concert venue. (Courtesy of Trevor Naylor)

Below: St George's modern extension. (Courtesy of Trevor Naylor)

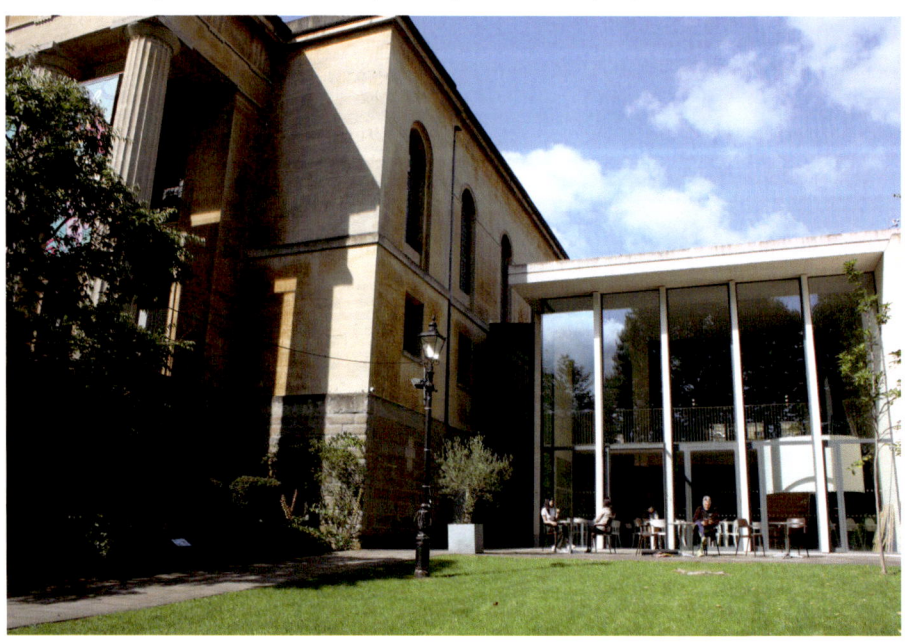

The church was built between 1821 and 1823 in thanksgiving for the Duke of Wellington's victory over Napoleon at the Battle of Waterloo eight years earlier; it is sometimes referred to as a 'Waterloo Church'. Its location was chosen because of the growing number of people moving into the Georgian houses being built in the streets around the church. Sir Robert Smirke, one of three Crown architects who were commissioned to design seven 'Waterloo' churches around the country, drew up the plans for the Church of St George. He made good use of the sloping site by creating a dramatic flight of steps on the church's south side. At the top of the steps, Sir Robert created a portico supported by four Doric columns.

In the enemy air raids of the Second World War an incendiary bomb hit the roof of the church, but fortunately it did not explode. A star-shaped ceiling light marks the spot where the bomb crashed into the main body of the church.

The death of Revd Percy Gay, who had served at St George's Church for forty-five years, along with crumbling fabric and a dwindling congregation, led to the church being declared redundant in 1984. At the time nearby homes were being vacated by their owners and were converted into offices and various departments for nearby Bristol University.

Being acoustically perfect, the church has been converted into a music centre known simply as St George's. It has become one of the best-known chamber concert halls in the country and performances by some of the world's greatest musicians are often broadcast from St George's by the BBC.

20. St Peter's Church, Bishopsworth

Standing in its spacious churchyard, this church has the atmosphere of being in a country village, yet it is only just over 2 miles south-west of Bristol's bustling city centre. The history of St Peter's Church is fascinating to say the least. There are records of the foundation of a church in Bishopsworth in 1194 that was a chapel of ease to Bedminster Parish Church, around a mile or so to the south.

The twelfth-century church at Bishopsworth was a small chapel, but it did not have a resident clergy team. Instead, churchgoers relied upon the services of a chaplain from Bedminster visiting them every Wednesday, Friday and Sunday. This arrangement seems to have continued until 1540 when the chapel was converted into three cottages. The cottages existed until Bristol City Council had them demolished in 1961 to make way for a swimming pool.

In the early nineteenth century, a room in the Georgian Bishopsworth Manor House (still standing) was consecrated so that church services could be held there.

In 1841 work started on building a permanent St Peter's Church. This took two years to construct, although its planned tower was never finished. St Peter's Church was built in a neo-Norman style and became a parish church in 1853. Many of its interior fittings and fixtures are of a Norman style and include a reredos and the font.

A clock was installed in the church tower in 1913 as a memorial to Revd Walter Molesworth, vicar of St Peter's for forty-one years (1868–1909). Before arriving in Bishopsworth, Revd Molesworth had served fourteen years at churches in Lincoln and Painswick in Gloucestershire.

English Heritage has designated St Peter's a Grade II* listed building.

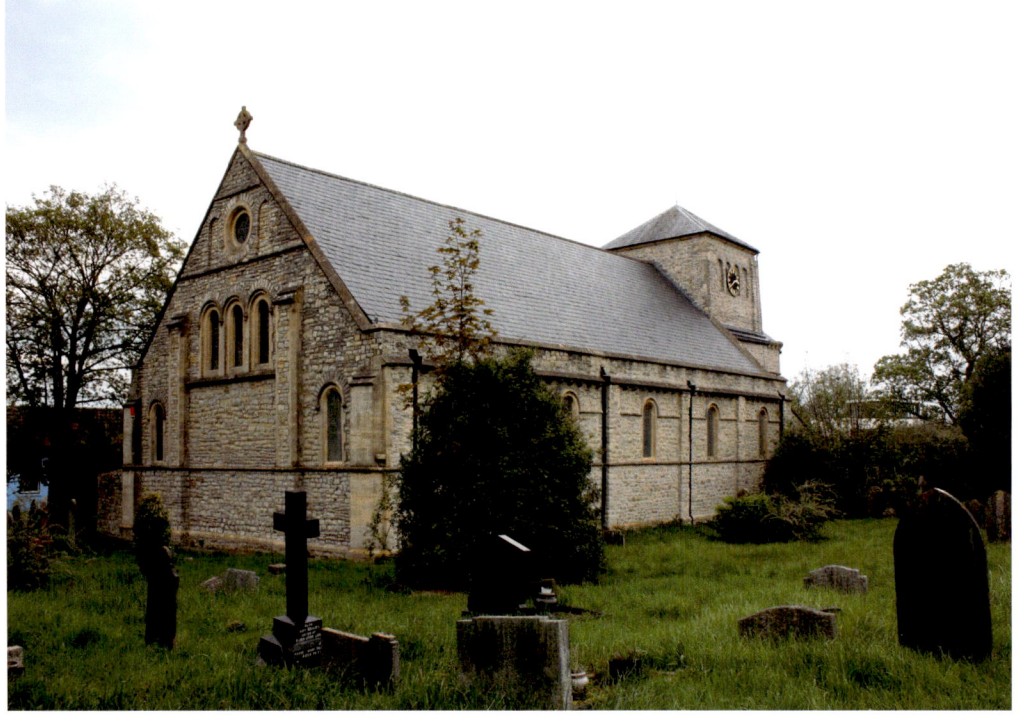

St Peter's Church, Bishopsworth. (Courtesy of Trevor Naylor)

21. St Michael the Archangel on the Mount Without, St Michael's Hill

The dedication of this church might be a mouthful to say, but it reflects its location on St Michael's Hill, which was outside of the old city walls when it was built. There has been a church on this site, at the bottom of one of Bristol's steepest hills, since around 1147. The 120-foot-high tower, which was added in the fifteenth century, overlooks the city centre. The bells were installed in 1737. Towards the end of the eighteenth century the church was said to be in such a ruinous condition that everything except the tower was demolished and rebuilt. The population of St Michael's Hill was also increasing, however, so consequently the church building needed to be enlarged.

In the Second World War a fire caused by incendiary bombs destroyed the church roof, but it was replaced a few years later.

Falling service attendance meant that St Michael's was made redundant and deconsecrated in 1991, which meant the end of one of the oldest and most unusual church traditions in the city. This was a candlelight service where the proceedings, including Bible readings, the Lord's Prayer and the sermon, were all said in Welsh. The special service was in honour of St David's Day and had been held for more than 250 years.

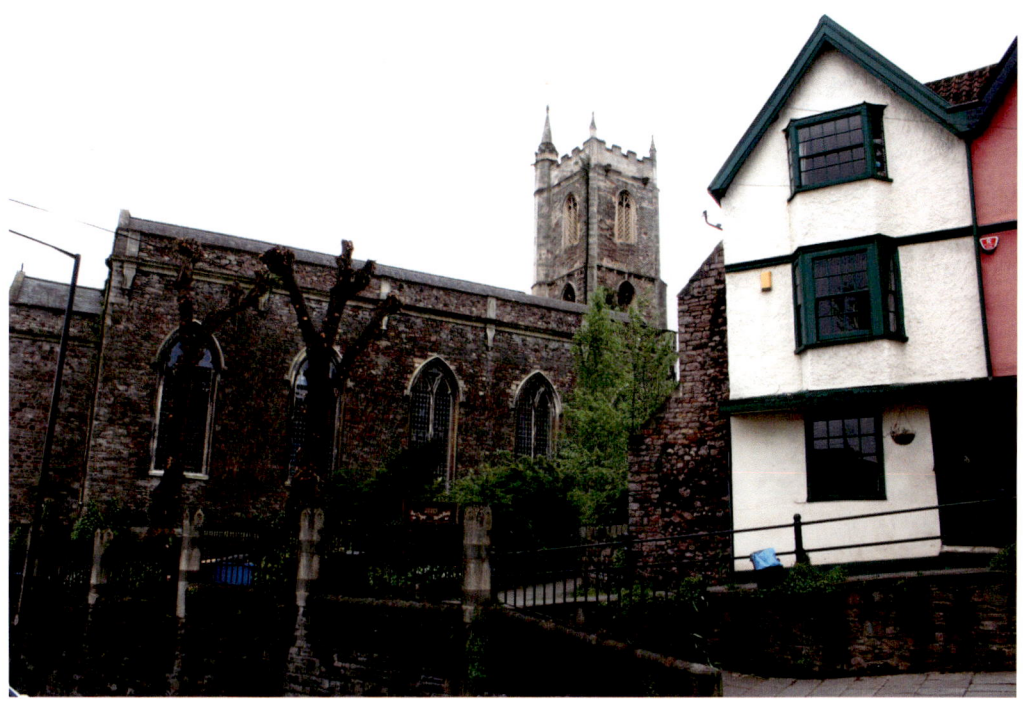

Above: St Michael-on-the-Mount-Without. (Courtesy of Trevor Naylor)

Below: St Michael-on-the-Mount-Without's clock. (Courtesy of Trevor Naylor)

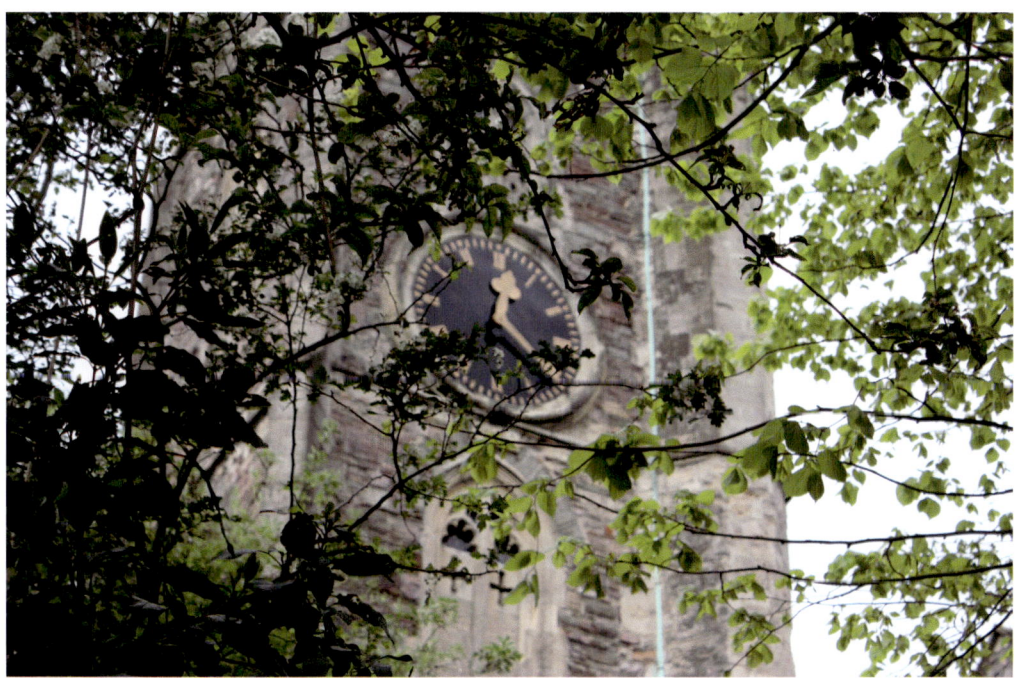

The empty church became virtually derelict and it was boarded up for many years. In 2016 the church was seriously damaged by fire. Fifteen fire engines attended the blaze; fire officers thought it was caused deliberately but no one has yet been found responsible, though it is believed that squatters in the church may have started it.

After negotiations with the diocese of Bristol, Norman Routledge, a local businessman, bought the remains of the church, which had been designated a Grade II* listed building by English Heritage. Norman Routledge has completely renovated St Michael's and transformed the church into a creative and performance space.

Remarkably, memorial plaques bearing the names of more than 800 soldiers of the 6th Battalion of the Gloucestershire Regiment who were killed in the First World War escaped damage during the blaze and have been removed from their original location in the church and installed in the crypt.

22. St Stephen's Church, St Stephen's Avenue

St Stephen's Church is the parish church of Bristol and has one of the biggest parish boundaries in the diocese – this includes all of the water (not the land areas alongside) the River Avon to the islands of Steep Holm and Flat Holm in the Severn Estuary.

The church is mentioned in documents as early as 1304, when it came under Glastonbury Abbey. Benedictine monks were the patrons of St Stephen's Church until the Dissolution of the Monasteries by Henry VIII. The abbot and parishioners of St Stephen's rebuilt the church in the fifteenth century. A wealthy merchant, John Shipward, Mayor of Bristol in 1455 and lived in a grand house near the church, paid for the elegant Perpendicular tower which rises 133 feet without the pinnacles. It is often regarded as one of the most handsome church towers in England.

When the River Frome was diverted in the thirteenth century, the harbour in the centre of Bristol was created. It resulted in St Stephen's Church standing on the quayside with ships moored so close that their masts were almost touching the church walls. This harbour church is known to have blessed ships that set out from Bristol from the thirteenth century onwards. The church is now surrounded by office blocks, cafés, shops, public houses and student accommodation.

An entry in the church's vestry book dated 27 November 1703 refers to what became known as the Great Storm. It started shortly after midnight and lasted five hours. According to the book: 'The like of the storm was never before known, it having blown down three (of the four) pinnacles from the tower, with all the battlements and clock, most of which fell fell through the roof of the southward and middle aisles into the body of the church, destroying abundance of the seats and pews; not sparing the windows and pillars.' The vestry book also notes that 6 inches of rain flooded the floor.

Being a harbour church, its fitting that St Stephen's should contain the tomb of Martin Pring, a mariner of much repute who was one of the earliest to attempt the discovery of a passage to the east by way of the Arctic Sea. Another tomb

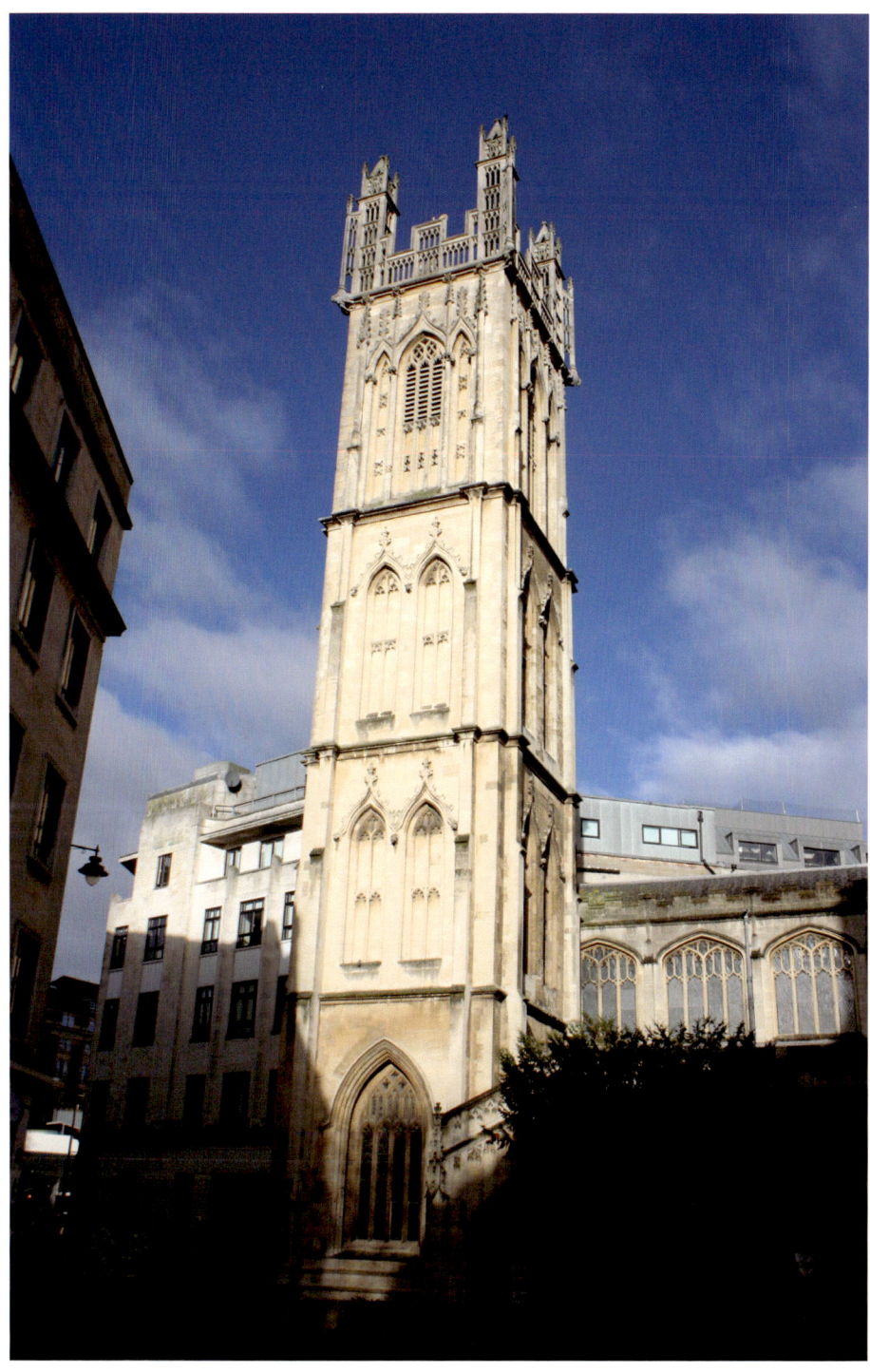

St Stephen's Church. (Courtesy of Trevor Naylor)

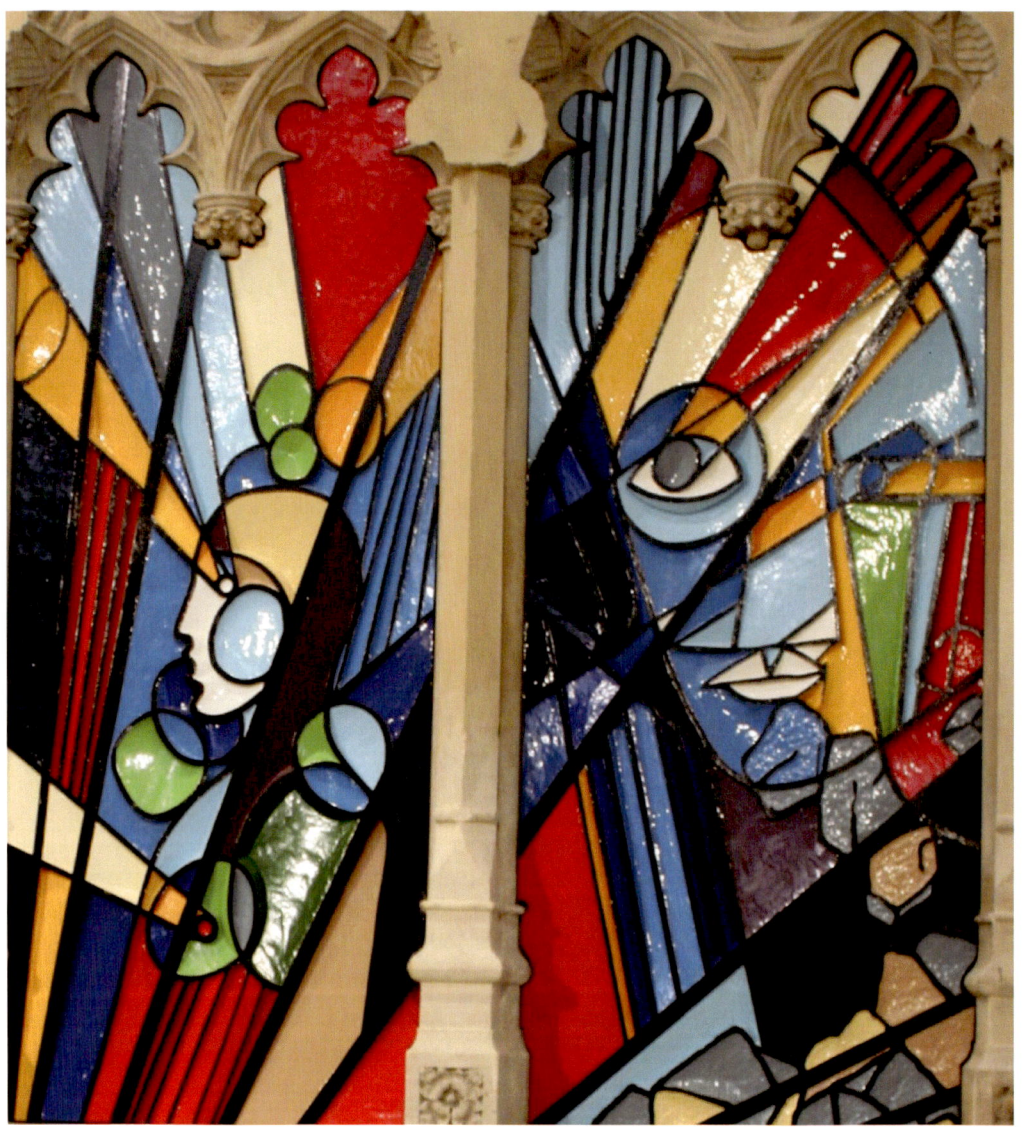

St Stephen's Church's artwork. (Courtesy of Trevor Naylor)

is attributed to be that of a fourteenth-century wool merchant named Edmund Blanket, who some say invented the blanket.

When Queen Elizabeth I visited Bristol in 1574 she was greeted by the ringing of the church bells by the Antient [sic] Society of St Stephen's Ringers. Apparently, she was so charmed by the efforts of the ringers that she promised them a royal warrant; it never materialised, however, and no one seems to know why. The society's members no longer ring the church's bells. That task fell some years ago to a new organisation called the St Stephen's Ringers Guild. The older

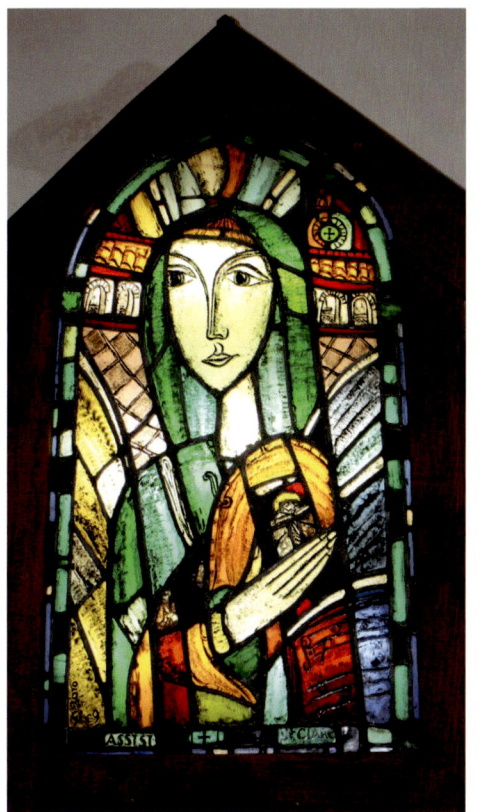 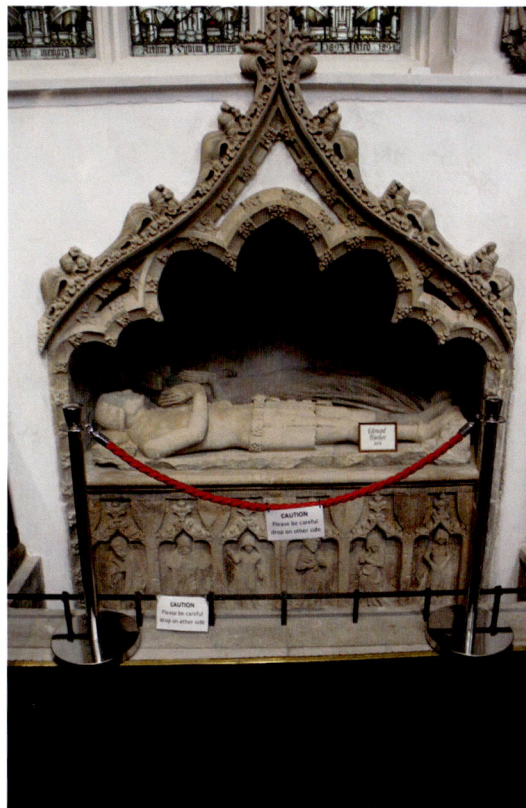

Above left: St Stephen's Church's artwork. (Courtesy of Trevor Naylor)

Above right: Tomb of Edmund Blanket. (Courtesy of Trevor Naylor)

body still plays an important role in the church's life by raising funds for the maintenance of its fabric. For reasons lost in the mists of time, the Antient Society of St Stephen's Ringers have always honoured Elizabeth I and on the Sunday nearest to her birthday, 17 November, they attend a special church service.

23. Holy Trinity Church, Westbury-on-Trym

It seems to be a little known fact that the suburb of Westbury-on-Trym is much older than Bristol itself. There was the church of a small monastery in existence at Westbury-on-Trym as far back as the eighth century. The church, built of wattle and daub, was dedicated to the Apostles Peter and Paul and built close to the River Trym. AD 717 is the accepted date of a Christian settlement here, hence the present Holy Trinity Church celebrated the 1,300th anniversary in 2017. A memorial window was created for the north aisle to mark this milestone in the number of years of Christian worship at Westbury-on-Trym.

In 1194 a college of priests that would go on for 300 years was set up, making Westbury an important ecclesiastical centre.

Construction of the present church began in the twelfth or early thirteenth century, though it has since been rebuilt several times. The oldest part is the arcade on the south side of the nave.

In the fifteenth century Bishop John Carpenter transformed the building into the Perpendicular style, adding a chancel. He had hopes that the church could be expanded and become a cathedral for the area, though this was not to be.

The boundary of Bristol was extended in 1904 to take in Westbury-on-Trym, which until then had been a rural village in Gloucestershire. It is 4 miles north of the centre of Bristol. The church was in the diocese of Worcester until the bishopric of Bristol was founded in 1542. From the large medieval parish of Westbury-on-Trym, fourteen modern Church of England parishes have been created in Bristol.

Holy Trinity Church stands on a mound in Church Road, its tower a prominent landmark overlooking the homes and shops that surround it. The church is a Grade I listed building and is the most historic building in Westbury-on-Trym.

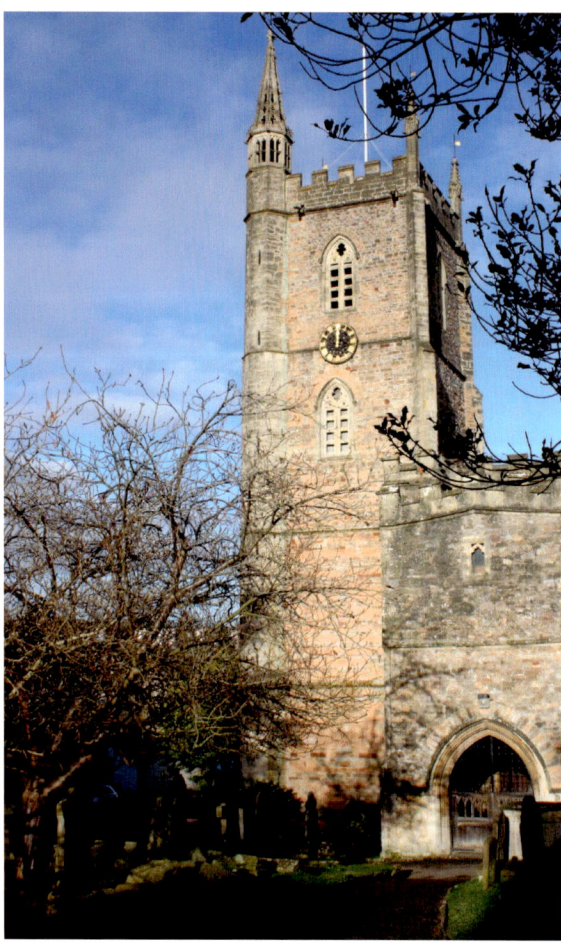

Holy Trinity Church, Westbury on Trym. (Courtesy of Trevor Naylor)

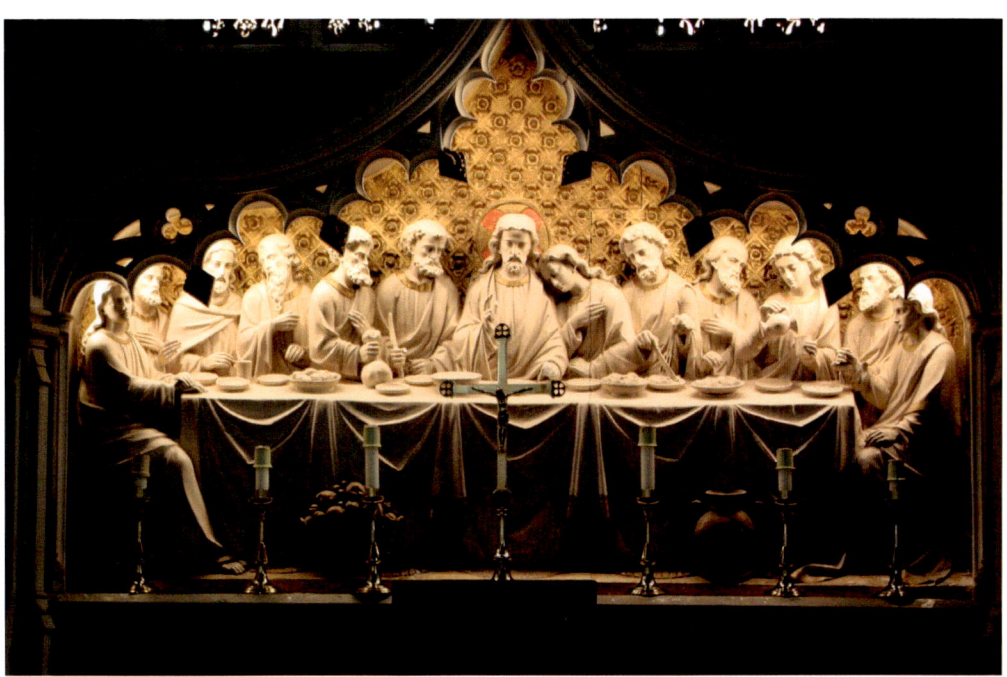

Above: Altarpiece, Holy Trinity Church. (Courtesy of Trevor Naylor)

Right: Stained-glass window, Holy Trinity Church. (Courtesy of Trevor Naylor)

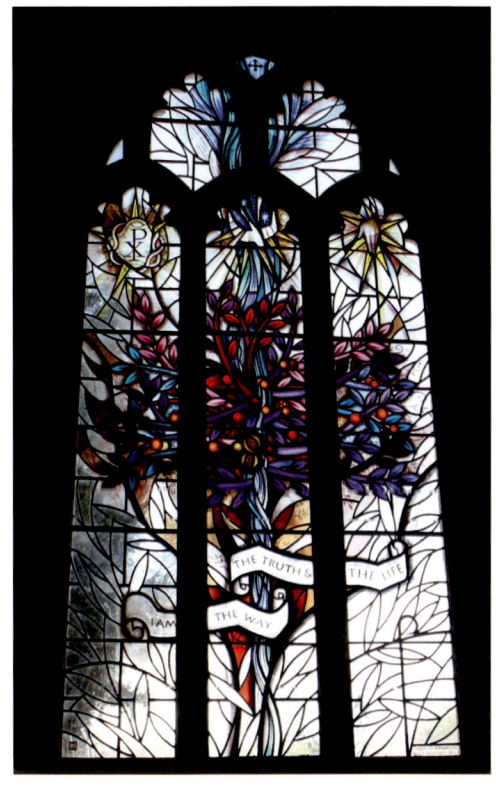

24. Bristol Cathedral, College Green

When King Henry VIII broke away from the papacy and appointed himself as Head of the Church of England, he dissolved all convents and monasteries and confiscated their revenues and any land that they may have held. In Bristol this included the suppression of St Augustine's Monastery and its abbey. This had been founded in 1140 by Robert Fitzharding, a reeve or provost of Bristol who later became the first Lord Berkeley. Fitzharding built the monastery just outside the original walls of Bristol on high ground that we now call College Green. This piece of open land, measuring just under 3 acres, now belongs to the dean and chapter of Bristol Cathedral. Fitzharding brought a group of Black Canons (Augustinians) from Herefordshire to Bristol to establish the abbey.

In 1542, three years after the dissolution, King Henry VIII created six new Church of England dioceses across the country, including one for Bristol, then England's second city after London. The king also gave Bristol a cathedral, which was formally dedicated as the Cathedral Church of the Holy and Undivided Trinity. It was the seat of the newly created Bishop of Bristol. For this post King Henry appointed one of his chaplains: Revd Paul Bush. He became one of the first bishops to marry, which resulted in him soon afterwards being deprived of his post. Bishop Bush's tomb can be found in the cathedral's eastern Lady Chapel.

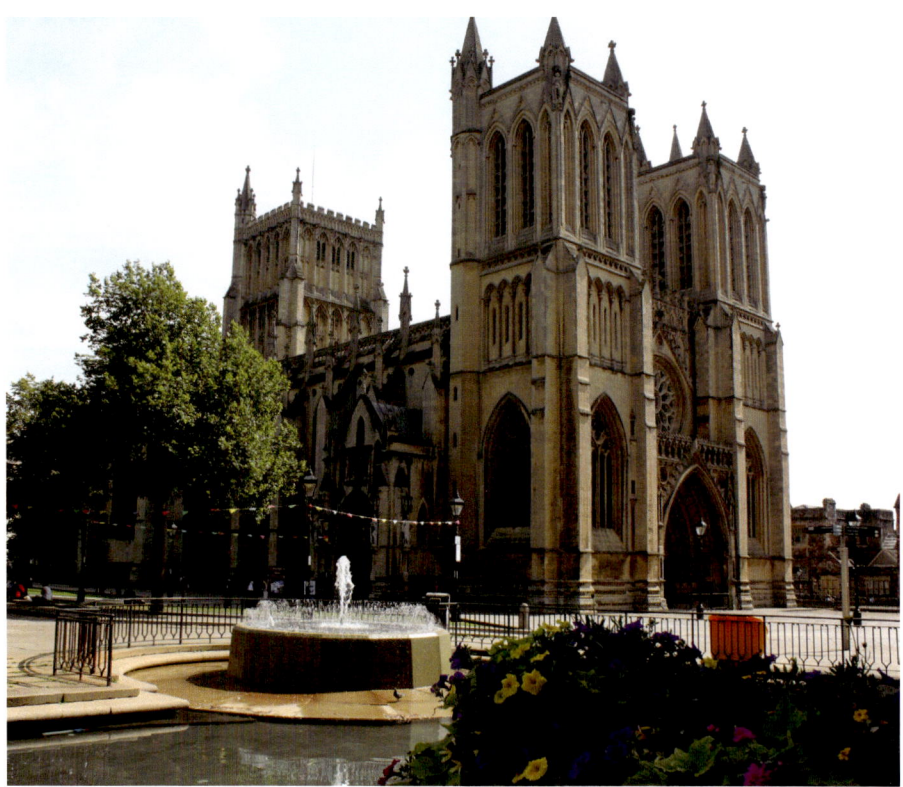

Bristol Cathedral. (Courtesy of Trevor Naylor)

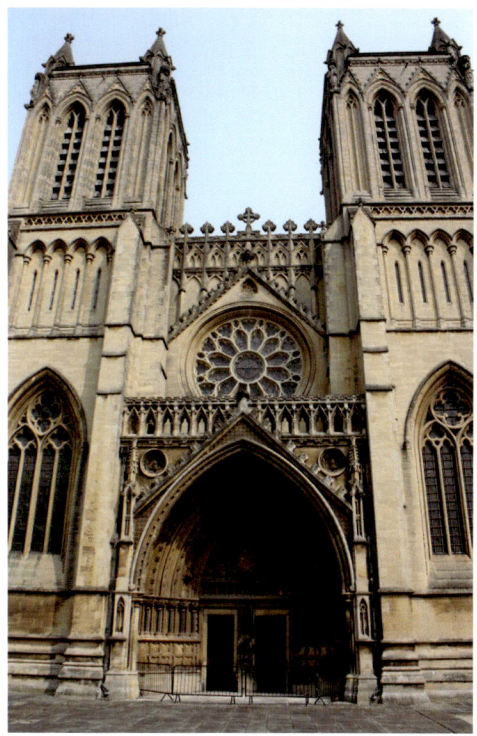

Right: Bristol Cathedral, great west door. (Courtesy of Trevor Naylor)

Below: Abbey gatehouse next to Bristol Cathedral. (Courtesy of Trevor Naylor)

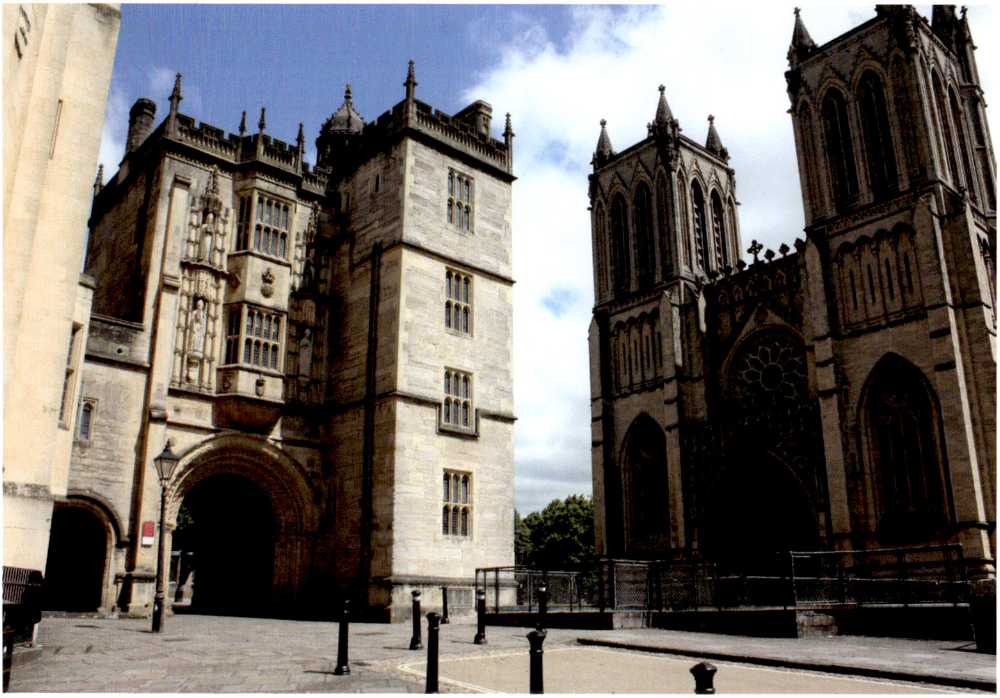

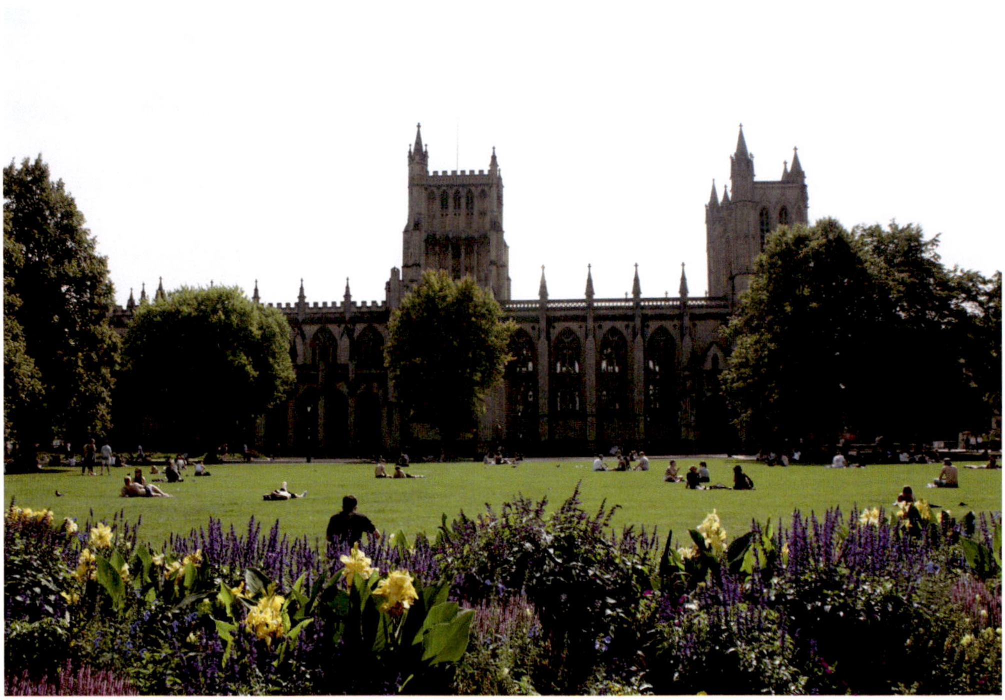

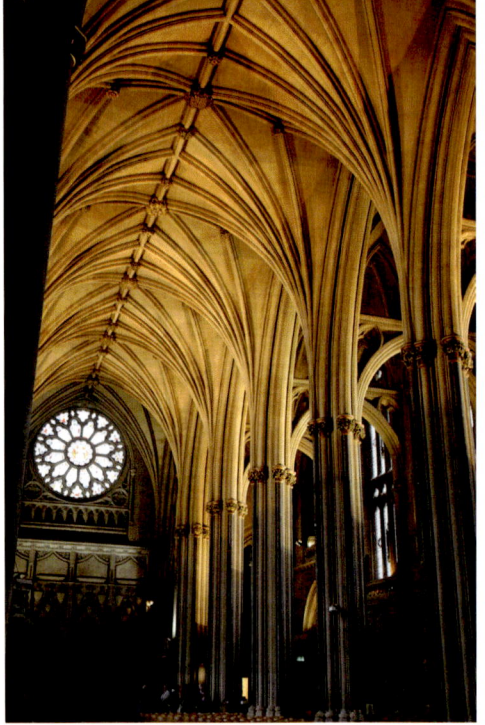

Above: Bristol Cathedral from College Green. (Courtesy of Trevor Naylor)

Left: Interior view. (Courtesy of Trevor Naylor)

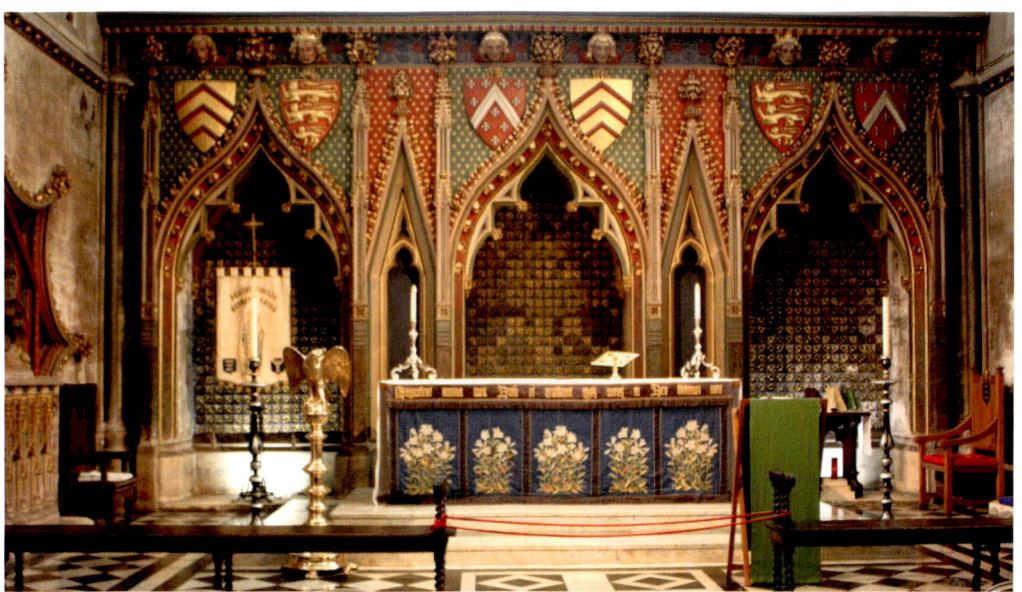

Above: Interior view. (Courtesy of Trevor Naylor)

Below: Window depicting the Red Cross. (Courtesy of Trevor Naylor)

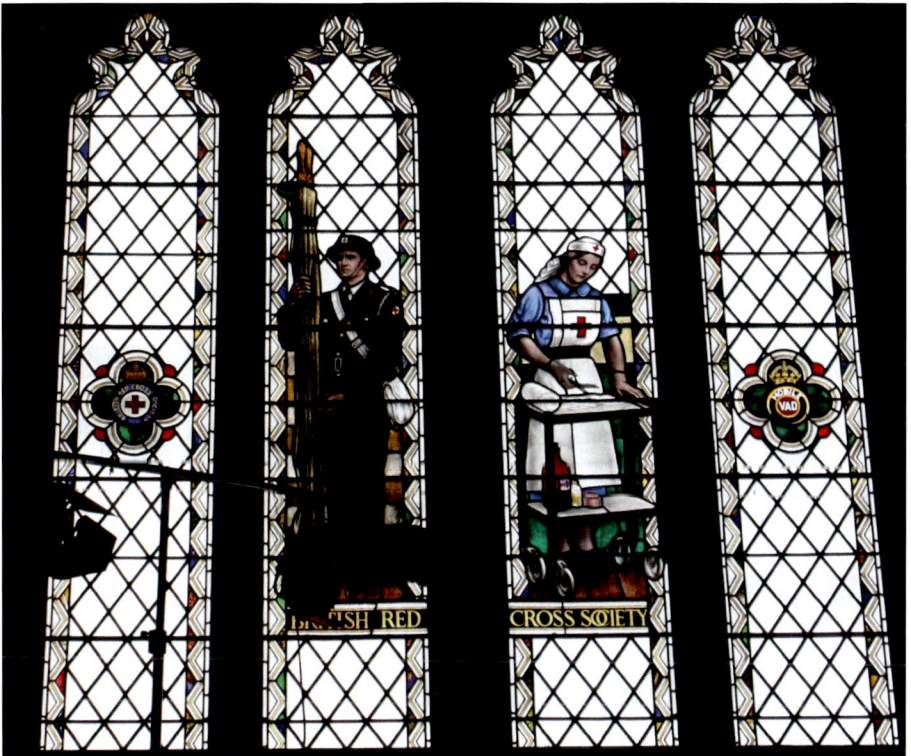

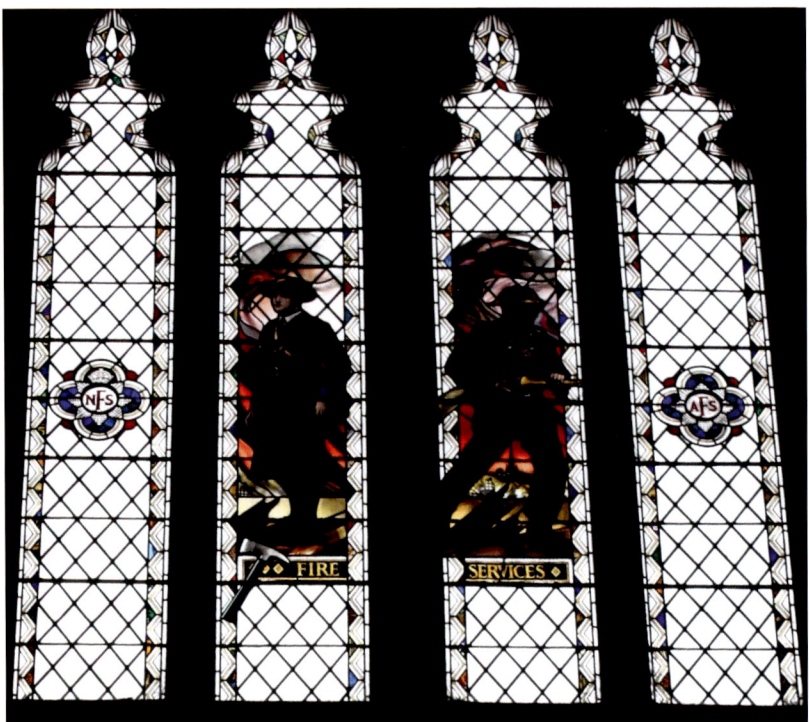

Above: Window depicting the fire service. (Courtesy of Trevor Naylor)

Below: Window depicting Bristol police. (Courtesy of Trevor Naylor)

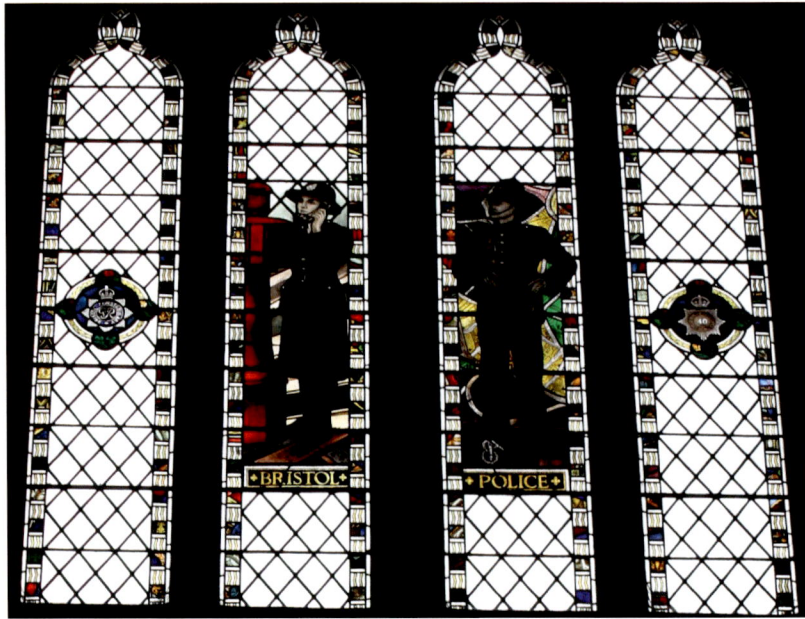

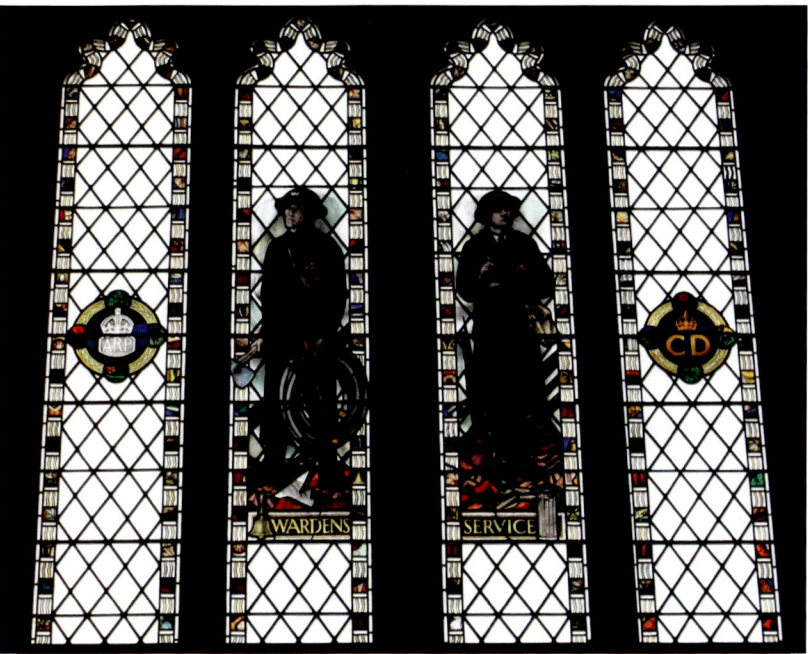

Above: Window depicting the Wardens Service. (Courtesy of Trevor Naylor)

Below: Window depicting the Home Guard. (Courtesy of Trevor Naylor)

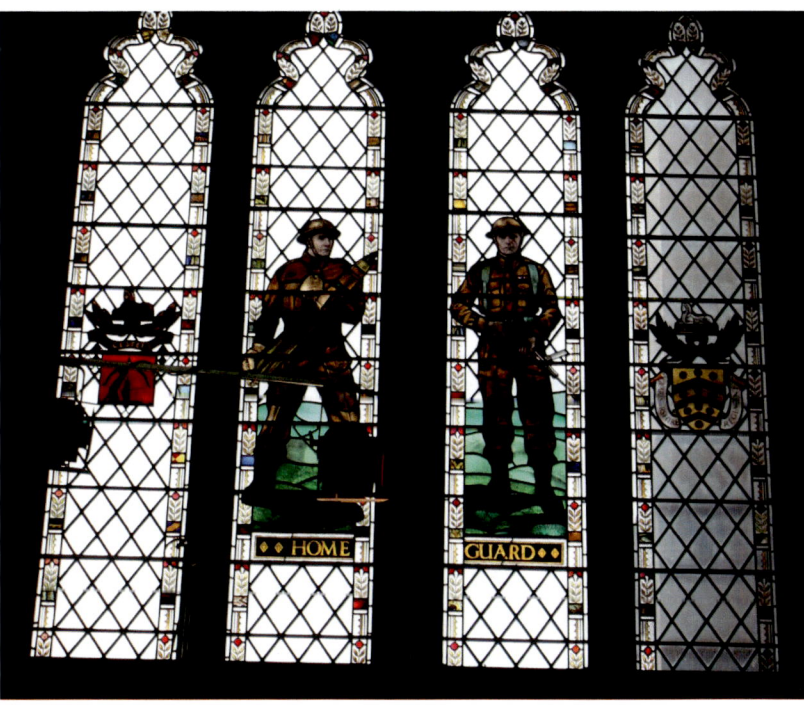

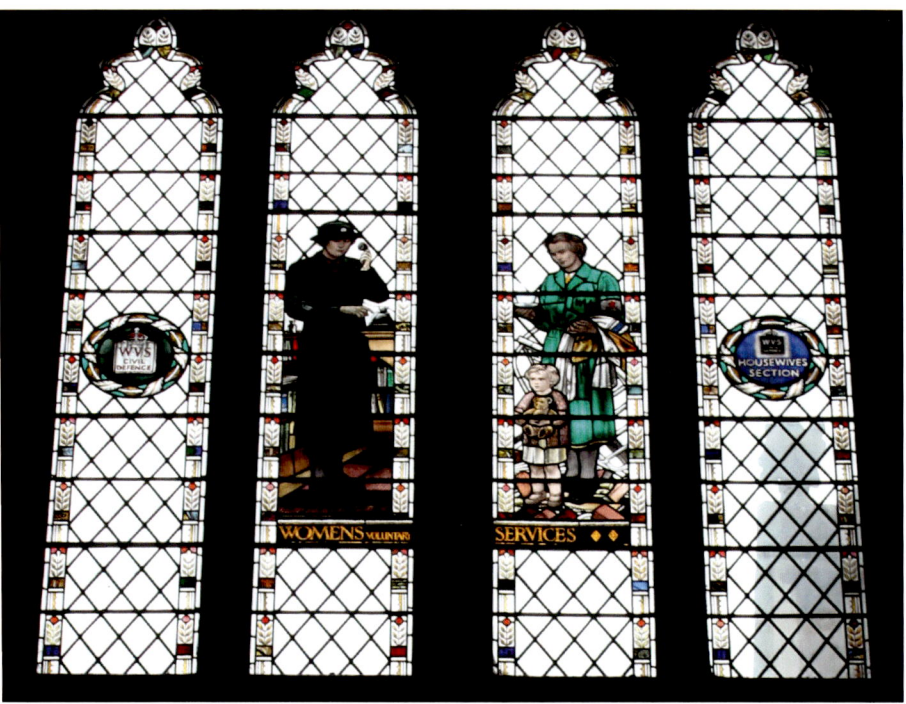

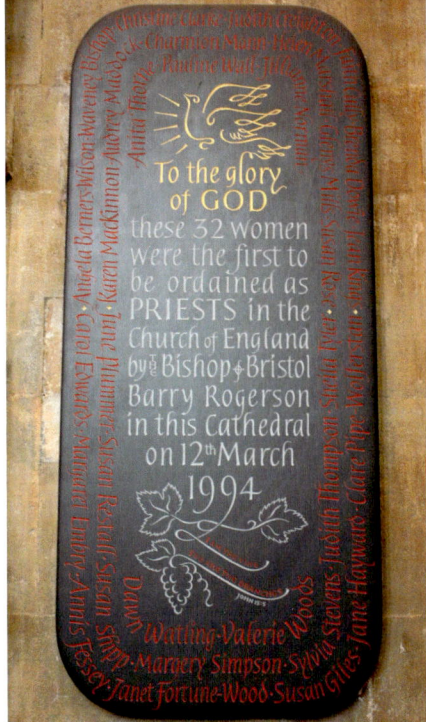

Above: Window depicting the Women's Voluntary Service. (Courtesy of Trevor Naylor)

Left: Plaque celebrating the first women ordained as priests in the Church of England. (Courtesy of Trevor Naylor)

At the dissolution of the monastery the nave of its church, which was to become the cathedral, was incomplete and pulled down. Readers will probably be surprised to learn that the new cathedral did not have a nave for 300 years. Its new one was built on the line of the old foundations, which were put in around 1500. The nave was completed during the last quarter of the nineteenth century at a cost of £77,447. Soon after, electric lighting was installed, making Bristol Cathedral the first cathedral to be lit by electricity. At around this time the quire screen separating the nave from the east end of the cathedral, the reredos (or screen behind the altar) and the pulpit were also added.

The remains of St Augustine's Abbey can still be seen in the chapter house (said to be one of the finest surviving Norman buildings in England), the abbey gatehouse and the buildings of Bristol Cathedral School. The gatehouse was once the main entrance to the abbey precinct. It stands between the cathedral and its neighbour, Bristol Central Library. The upper floor of the gatehouse was added in the fifteenth century and today the building is used as offices for the administration of the cathedral.

An unusual feature of the cathedral's architectural style is that it is a fine example of what is called a 'hall church'. This is where the vaulted ceilings of the nave, choir and aisle are all the same height. There is no other cathedral in England like it. Various styles of architecture can be found in the cathedral including Early English, Early Decorated, Decorated and Perpendicular.

Bomb damage in 1941 during the Second World War destroyed the windows in the cathedral's north nave aisle. They were replaced by windows that commemorate the work of the civilian forces to the war effort.

Bristol Cathedral made ecclesiastical history in 1994 when the first women were ordained into the Church of England priesthood within its hallowed walls. This was the culmination of the most bitterly fault battle within the Church since Henry VIII's Reformation. There was both support and opposition by churchmen and women from all parts of the Anglican Communion. One vicar requested his church bell should be tolled during the service of ordination. While protestors with placards stood outside the cathedral during this historic service, a team of vergers patrolled the congregation looking for potential troublemakers. In the event no problems occurred. Altogether, thirty-two women stood before the then Bishop of Bristol, the Rt Revd Barry Rogerson, to be ordained. The service was broadcast by television and radio crews to countries around the world, putting Bristol Cathedral firmly on the global stage.

25. ST MARY REDCLIFFF CHURCH, REDCLIFFE

Arguably, this is Bristol's most talked about and famous church. To say that it is worth exploration is an understatement. The Christian community has worshipped continuously on the site occupied by St Mary Redcliffe Church for nearly 900 years. The first church was probably built at Redcliffe in Saxon times, when Bristol first became a port. The original quayside was just across the road, below the red sandstone cliff from which this area gets its name. St Mary Redcliffe Church was originally at the very centre of the shipping industry, which is a key to its own history. Merchants from the port of Bristol,

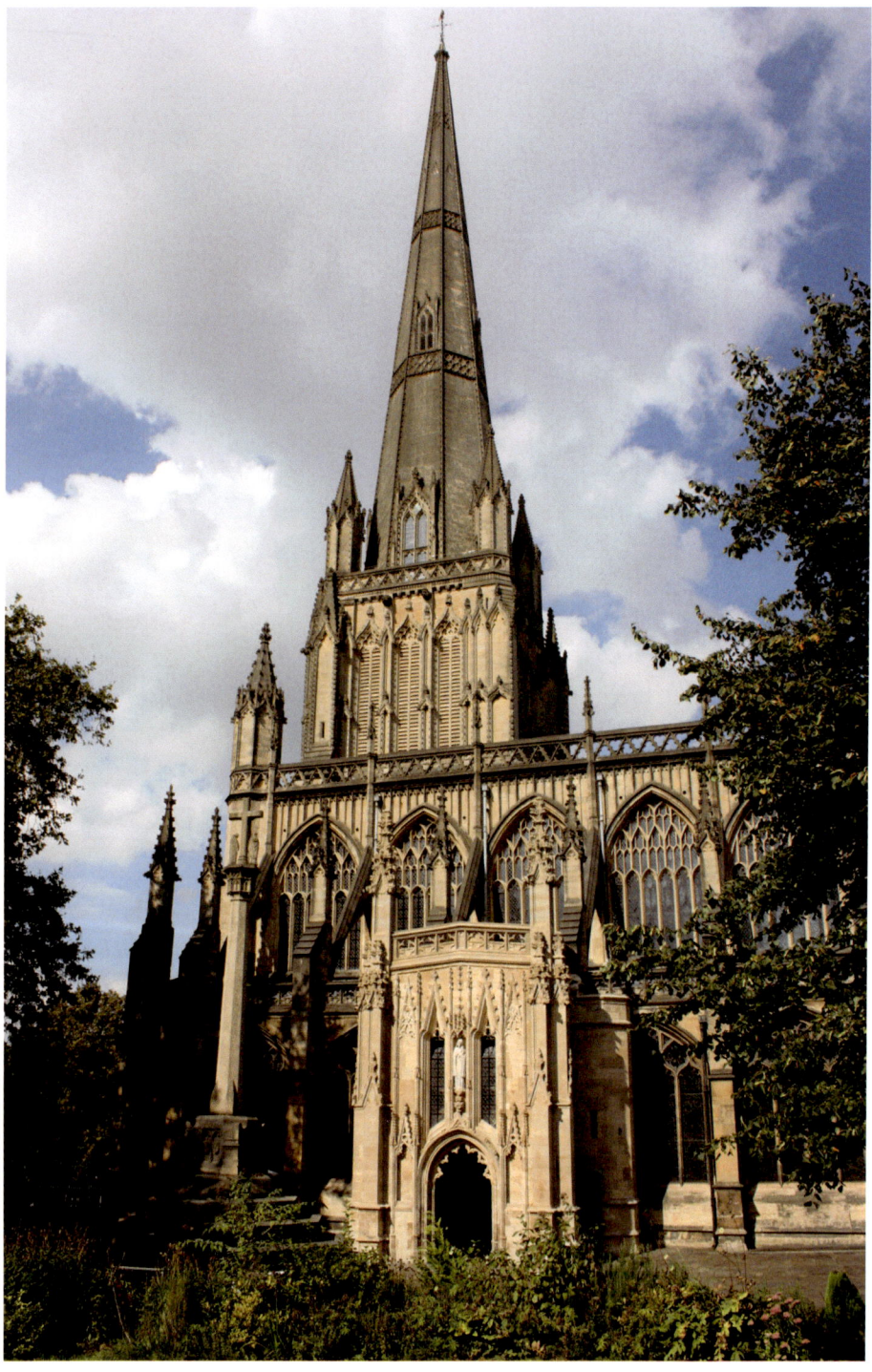

The dramatic St Mary Redcliffe. (Courtesy of Trevor Naylor)

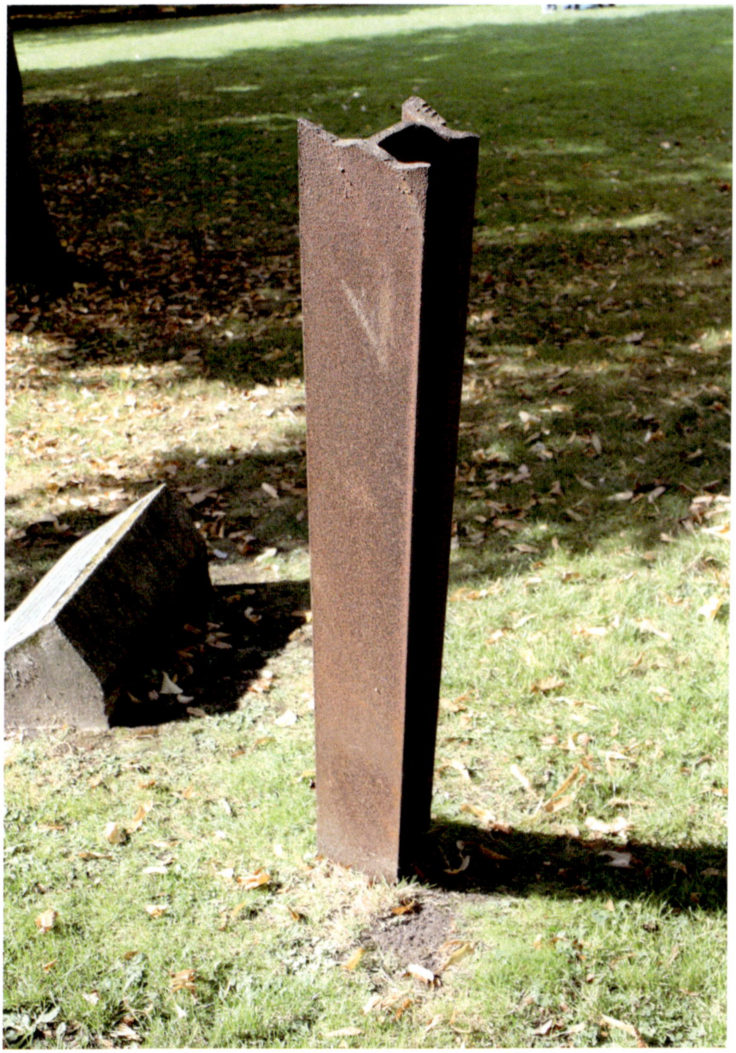

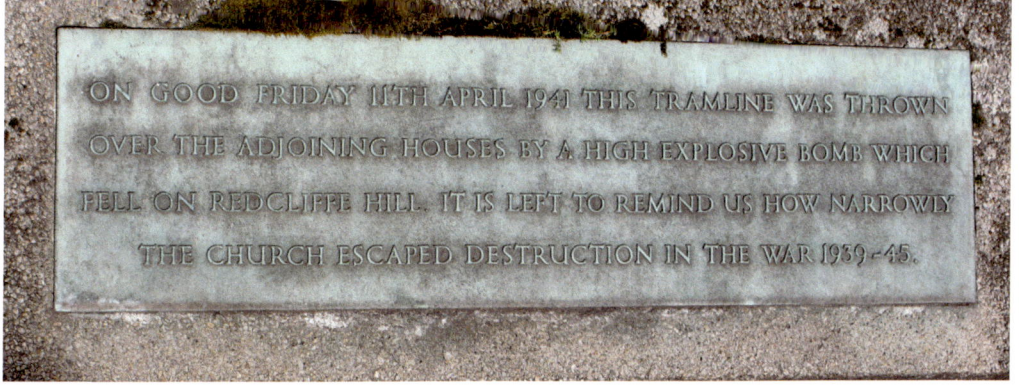

Right: A tramline embedded in St Mary Redcliffe's graveyard after an air raid. (Courtesy of Trevor Naylor)

Below: The tramline plaque. (Courtesy of Trevor Naylor)

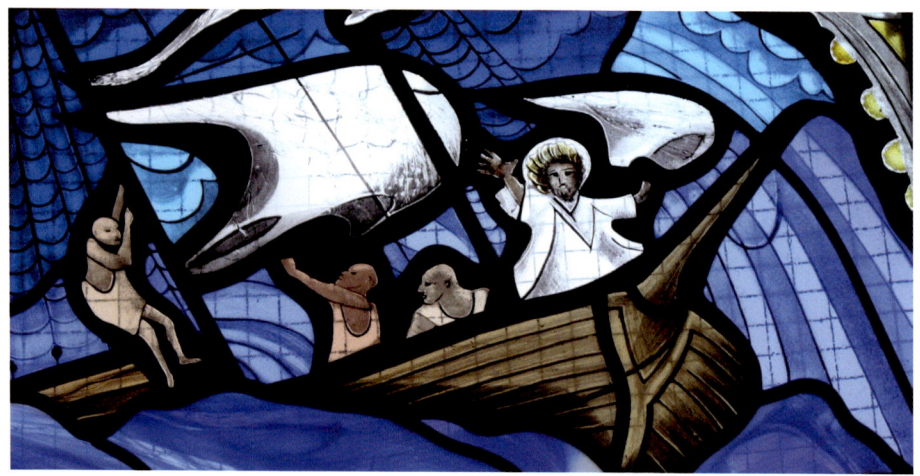
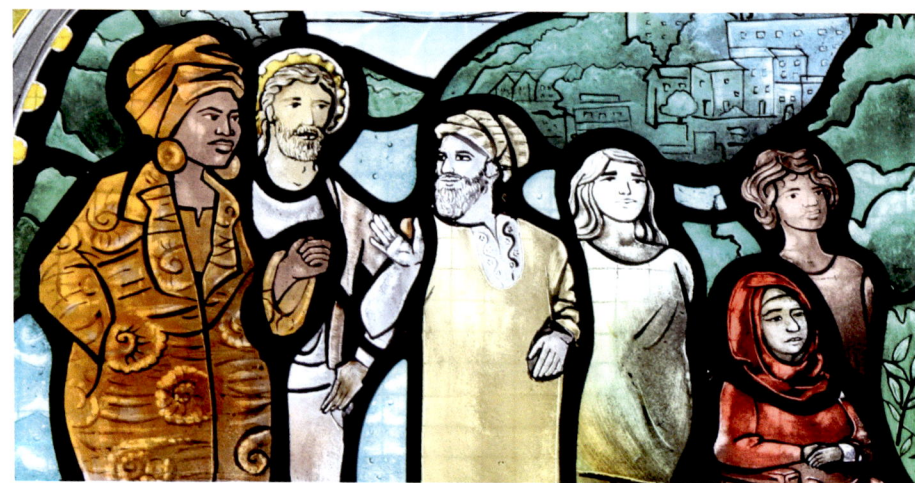
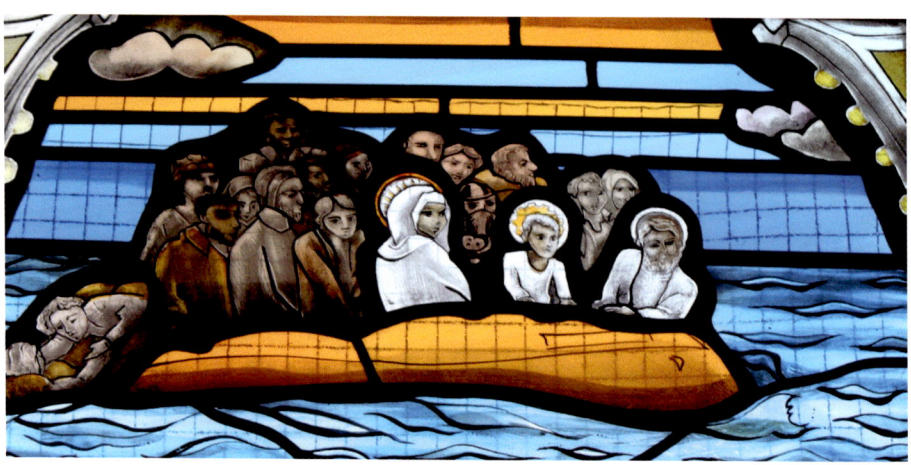

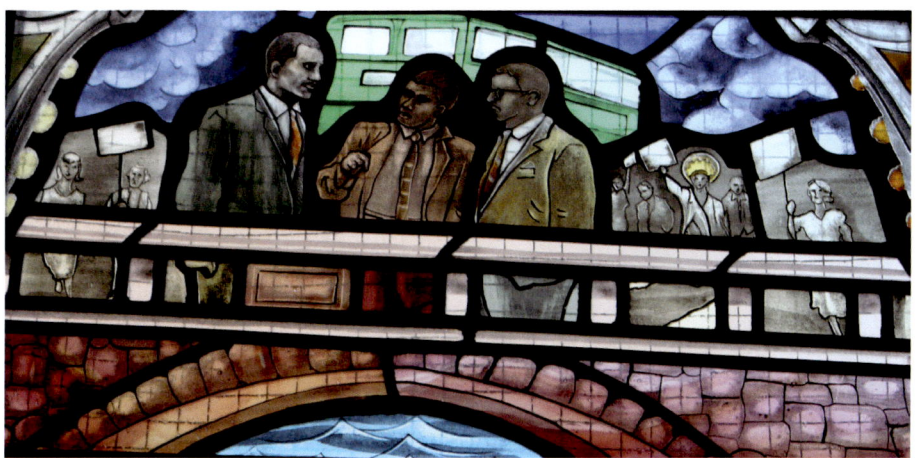

Above: Stained-glass window showing leaders of the Bristol bus boycott. (Courtesy of Trevor Naylor)

Opposite above: Stained-glass window showing Jesus as a black man. (Courtesy of Trevor Naylor)

Opposite middle: Stained-glass window showing Bristol people of heritage. (Courtesy of Trevor Naylor)

Opposite below: Stained-glass window showing refugees in a boat. (Courtesy of Trevor Naylor)

and possibly the explorer John Cabot, began and ended their voyages at the shrine of our Lady of Redcliffe.

With its grandeur, elegance and stately 'cloud-piercing' spire the church is often mistaken for a cathedral, but St Mary Redcliffe is a parish church.

The present church was largely built in the fourteenth and fifteenth centuries. Its transepts and choir date back to that period. William Canynge, a wealthy merchant and the owner of nine ships, spent a fortune on restoring the church. Unfortunately, a massive thunderstorm in 1445 brought about two-thirds of the spire crashing down. The principal entrance is through the north porch. The inner part of the porch dates from 1185 and is said to be the oldest part of the building. The outer porch was added some 150 years later.

The church could well be called 'Right Royal Redcliffe' on account of the many visits down the years by members of the royal family – probably far more than other churches. Queen Elizabeth I is reputed to have given the church its greatest accolade of all in describing it as 'the fairest, goodliest and most famous parish church in England'. However, no record has ever been found of her saying this; not even a mention in the church records. There is no evidence either that she visited the church during her visit to Bristol. Furthermore, the church was not at its architectural best when the queen was in the city in 1574 as its landmark spire would not be rebuilt for another 300 years.

When it was completed in 1872 the mayor of Bristol, Mr William Proctor, and the lady mayoress accepted a most unusual invitation from the vicar to lay the capstone almost 300 feet above street level. The ceremony was held on Ascension Day in 1872 with the spire encased in scaffolding. The *Bristol Times and Mirror* newspaper reported that the only way for the civic couple to reach the top was by a series of hoists. The newspaper reported: 'It was two square boards, one overhead and the other underfoot, like the top and bottom of a box with a rope at each corner, covered on three sides with drapery.'

The older a church is, the more likelihood there is of costly repairs to the building. Unlike many places of worship on the Continent, churches in England do not benefit from government grants. So, in 1848 the Canynge's Society of Friends of Redcliffe was formed to raise funds for the restoration of the church. The society's main objective at the time was to financially help towards the cost of rebuilding the spire. The society took its name from a wealthy medieval merchant, William Canynge, who in the fifteenth century adapted St Mary Redcliffe Church to its present form.

Just over a century after Elizabeth I was in Bristol, Charles I declared: 'The parish church of Redcliffe for the foundation structures and buildings thereof is one of the most absolute fairest and goodliest parish churches within the realm of England.'

A royal proclamation of 1660 ordered that the coat of arms of Charles II be set up in all parish churches. Many of them have long disappeared, but a colourful one made of stone can be found at St Mary Redcliffe above the south door.

Queen Elizabeth II made two visits to the church: once in 1956 and the second time in 1995. As she signed the Visitor's Book during her second visit, the queen told Revd Tony Whatmough that St Mary Redcliffe was 'not the sort of church that you forgot once you had visited it'.

The church's interior is particularly interesting for the many plaques and wall tablets which are memorials to some of Bristol's most famous residents of the past. Among the various artefacts are the armour and pennants of Sir William Penn, who became Vice Admiral of England. Contemporary writers described him as the most distinguished Bristolian of the seventeenth century. An artefact of a different kind is a whalebone said to have been brought back to Bristol by the maritime explorer John Cabot after he discovered Newfoundland in 1497. It takes pride of place on one of the walls.

Another distinctive feature are the 1,000 (or perhaps more) gilded bosses in the roof vaulting, all of which are believed to be different. They include a maze, green men, a monster biting its own tail and a mermaid with traditional long tresses holding a comb in one hand and a mirror in the other.

Fortunately, St Mary Redcliffe escaped serious damage in the Second World War. However, a tramline lies deeply embedded in the south churchyard, where it landed during an air raid. The vicar of the church at the time said it should remain there as a reminder of how close the church came to being destroyed. He said it would also remind people of 'the horrors of war'.

The size and beauty of the church makes it an ideal venue for many special events, like the annual Rush Sunday service where the floor of the nave is strewn with rushes picked from the Somerset moors and mixed with herbs and bay leaves. The lord mayor and councillors take part in the 500-year-old tradition in scarlet robes along with many other civic dignitaries.

The church made national headlines in 2024 when it replaced a stained-glass window that commemorated the Bristol-born slave trader Edward Colston, who is now out of favour due to his connections to the Atlantic slave trade. It was replaced with windows depicting Jesus in a number of different situations, including joining the Bristol Bus Boycott, on a Bristol ship on a slaving voyage, as a child refugee fleeing to Egypt and among a diverse group of neighbours. The windows were designed by the local Dr Ealish Swift to counter the Anglo-centric narrative of a white Jesus.

26. St Werburgh's Church, St Werburgh's

If only the hallowed walls of Bristol's oldest churches could talk, we would most likely hear many fascinating and unusual tales, not just about churches but also the city's history. Take, for example, the medieval church of St Werburgh's. No records have ever been found stating when the church was first built, but it is believed to have been founded in the late twelfth century. It originally stood in the oldest area of Bristol, on the corner of Corn Street and Small Street. It was rebuilt in 1758 and demolished later to be rebuilt elsewhere in the city.

According to *Arrowsmith's Dictionary of Bristol*, which was published in 1906, not a single ratepayer in 1871 lived in the area around St Werburgh's Church. A movement is said to have sprung up for the removal of the church to a 'necessitous suburban district'. Another account claims that the church had to be removed because it caused the road to narrow and large horse-drawn carriages were causing much congestion.

One of the worshippers at St Werburgh's was John Foster, a wealthy salt merchant who was mayor of Bristol in 1481. He was the founder of the Three Kings of Cologne Chapel at the top of Christmas Steps.

Whatever the reason, an Act of Parliament was needed to remove a church, and this was obtained by the church authorities in 1875. Work began on dismantling St Werburgh's Church stone by stone two years later. Each stone was numbered to make it easier to reconstruct the church in Perpendicular Gothic Revival style. The stones were hauled by some of the sturdiest horses in Bristol just under 2 miles to Mina Road. The area was then renamed after the church. The first services at the 'new' St Werburgh's Church were held on 30 September 1879. It is unclear why a Bristol church should be dedicated to St Werburgh, an Anglo-Saxon princess who later became patron saint of the city of Chester.

While the church in Corn Street was being taken down 100 lead coffins and four large chests of human remains were transferred to Greenbank Cemetery in east Bristol.

The diocese of Bristol declared St Werburgh's Church redundant in 1988 as its small congregation could no longer financially support the building. The last service to be held there was on Remembrance Sunday 1988.

The church has been designated by English Heritage as a Grade II* building. Its interior has become Bristol's first indoor climbing centre and is known simply as 'The Church'. One of its features is the main wall, which climbs into the tower. Some church furnishings still remain, including an octagonal pulpit, choir stalls and sculptures, but for the sake of safety they are behind specially installed

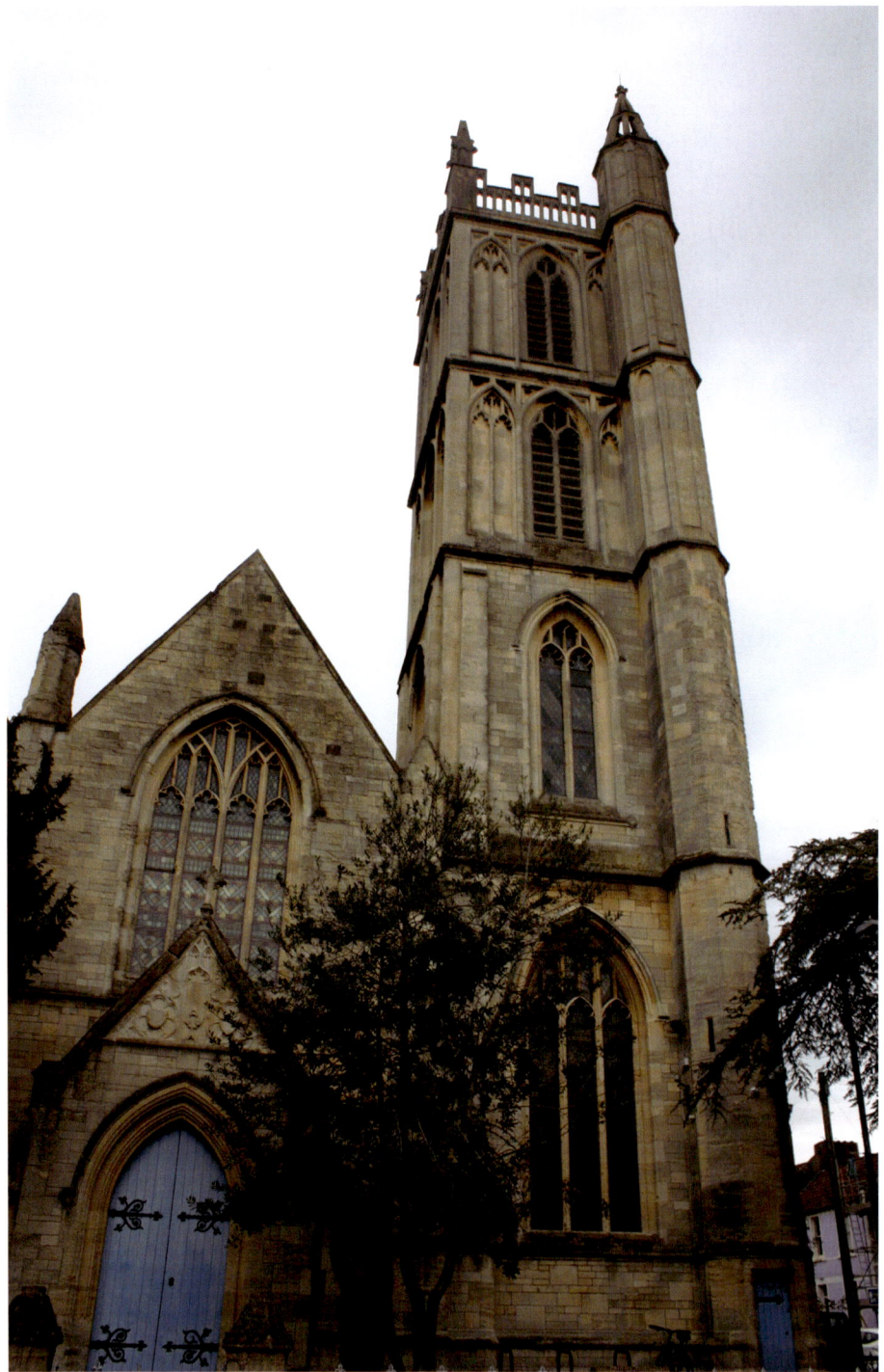

St Werburgh's Church. (Courtesy of Trevor Naylor)

climbing walls. The church also has many plaques on its walls in memory of people who worshipped there.

With its imposing 80-foot-high tower, St Werburgh's is still a local landmark. The diocese of Bristol stipulated that the building should not be altered in case it was ever wanted again as a church.

27. St Paul's Church, St Paul's

St Paul's Church is the centrepiece of Portland Square, which was laid out in the eighteenth century as part of one of Bristol's earliest suburbs. The square itself became a residential area for wealthy merchants. The church was designed by local architect Daniel Hague and the first service held there was appropriately enough on St Paul's Day in 1794.

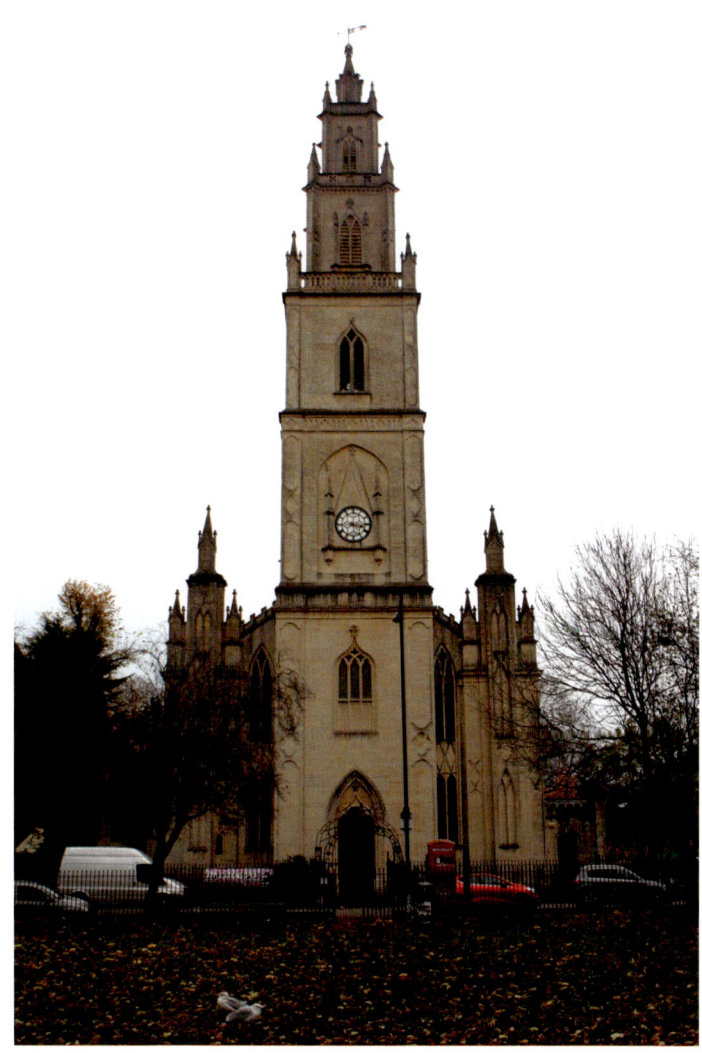

St Paul's Church, known as the 'wedding cake'. (Courtesy of Trevor Naylor)

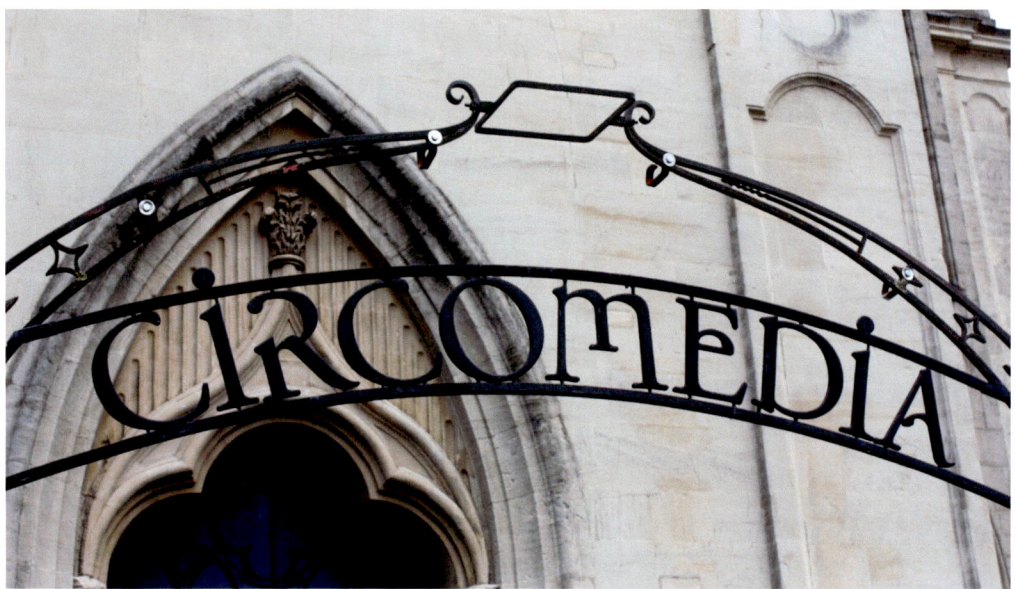

St Paul's Church, now a performance space. (Courtesy of Trevor Naylor)

The church has long been affectionately known by Bristolians as the 'wedding cake' church on account of its unusual, tiered tower at the west front. The tower was designed to hold a peal of ten bells but only four were purchased, which were all cast at a foundry in Gloucester. The architectural style of the church is Gothic blended with a classical look. It is in vast contrast to the modern style of the nearby late twentieth-century Cabot shopping centre.

St Paul's Church is on the National Heritage List for England and ranked as a Grade I listed building. Its gates and railings also appear on the list as Grade II*. Although the church is no longer a place of worship, the building still has an ornate Georgian plaster ceiling, stone columns and a wealth of stained glass.

One of the earliest performances in Bristol of Handel's *Messiah* is said to have taken place in St Paul's Church. It was performed by a 120-strong orchestra and choir at what was called a 'grand musical festival' which was raising funds for the Bristol Infirmary.

As people living in Portland Square moved out of the area into other parts of the city, especially the up-and-coming district of Clifton with its Georgian squares and crescents, the church's congregation became smaller and smaller. Eventually the diocese of Bristol closed St Paul's Church in 1988. Through disuse, the building fell into disrepair. The Heritage Lottery Fund gave the Bristol diocese more than £2 million so that repairs could be carried out. The building was also converted into its present use as the home of Circomedia, a circus school which is equipped with items such as aerial and trapeze equipment.

Only one of the church's four bells now remains in the tower. The others have gone to churches in the farming village of Buckland Dinham in Somerset, Wagga Wagga in New South Wales and Sydney, Australia.

28. St Mary Magdalene, Stoke Bishop

'Picturesque' is often a word that is overused, but on this occasion it is appropriate. You enter the churchyard of St Mary Magdalene through a lychgate on Mariners Drive, which has surely been the background for many newlyweds' photographs.

St Mary Magdalene Church stands in the heart of the leafy and affluent suburb of Stoke Bishop. It is bordered by the roughly 400 acres of Clifton and Durdham Downs and the River Trym. At the time the church was built in the second half of the nineteenth century, Stoke Bishop was part of the county of Gloucestershire. It wasn't until 1904 that it was absorbed into the city of Bristol.

Meanwhile, a certain number of 'resident gentry' felt that to go their nearest parish church at Westbury-on-Trym, a round journey of 3 miles, was inconvenient to say the least. They had to follow tracks that were not only bumpy but often muddy, particularly in the winter. A movement got going to build a church at Stoke Bishop. A local builder, William Baker, gave some scrubland he owned as the site on which it could be erected. He also made a generous contribution of £250 towards the cost of the church. There were also monetary gifts from other people living in Stoke Bishop. The new parish of Stoke Bishop was carved out of the Westbury-on-Trym parish.

St Mary Magdalene Church was designed in a plain style by John Norton, a highly respected architect who was born in Bristol but moved to London. In the capital he developed a large architectural practice in designing both country houses and ecclesiastical buildings. He frequently returned to Bristol as he was commissioned to design a number of churches in the city as well as a training college for the Gloucester and Bristol diocese – the two dioceses were linked at the time. The foundation stone of St Mary's was laid in 1858 and the building was completed two years later. At the time the church was surrounded by fields, some of which were used by sheep grazing. What was open land is largely covered today by a mixture of manor-style houses with gardens, large villas and purpose-built blocks of flats.

In 1871 the nave of St Mary's was extended and the west porch added. The tower and spire were also erected, which would complete John Norton's original plan for the church. The spire rose 160 feet above street level. It was nearly destroyed when a storm brought it crashing down, but fortunately the spire fell away from the church. Although the builders were on the site at the time, no one was injured. A collection was taken for repairs and about a year later the spire was completed. In 1883 a clock was placed in the tower, the chancel extended and a south aisle chapel added. The lychgate was dedicated in December 1919 as a memorial to two men – one aged twenty-five, the other aged twenty-three – who lost their lives while on service in the First World War.

Pew rentals were introduced by many churches as a way of boosting church funds. Despite having many wealthy people in the congregation, St Mary's was no exception. Records show that in the mid-1920s this source of annual income was bringing in more than £400 a year. However, the church council decided that from Easter Day 1939 all pews would be free. St Mary's Church is a Grade II listed building.

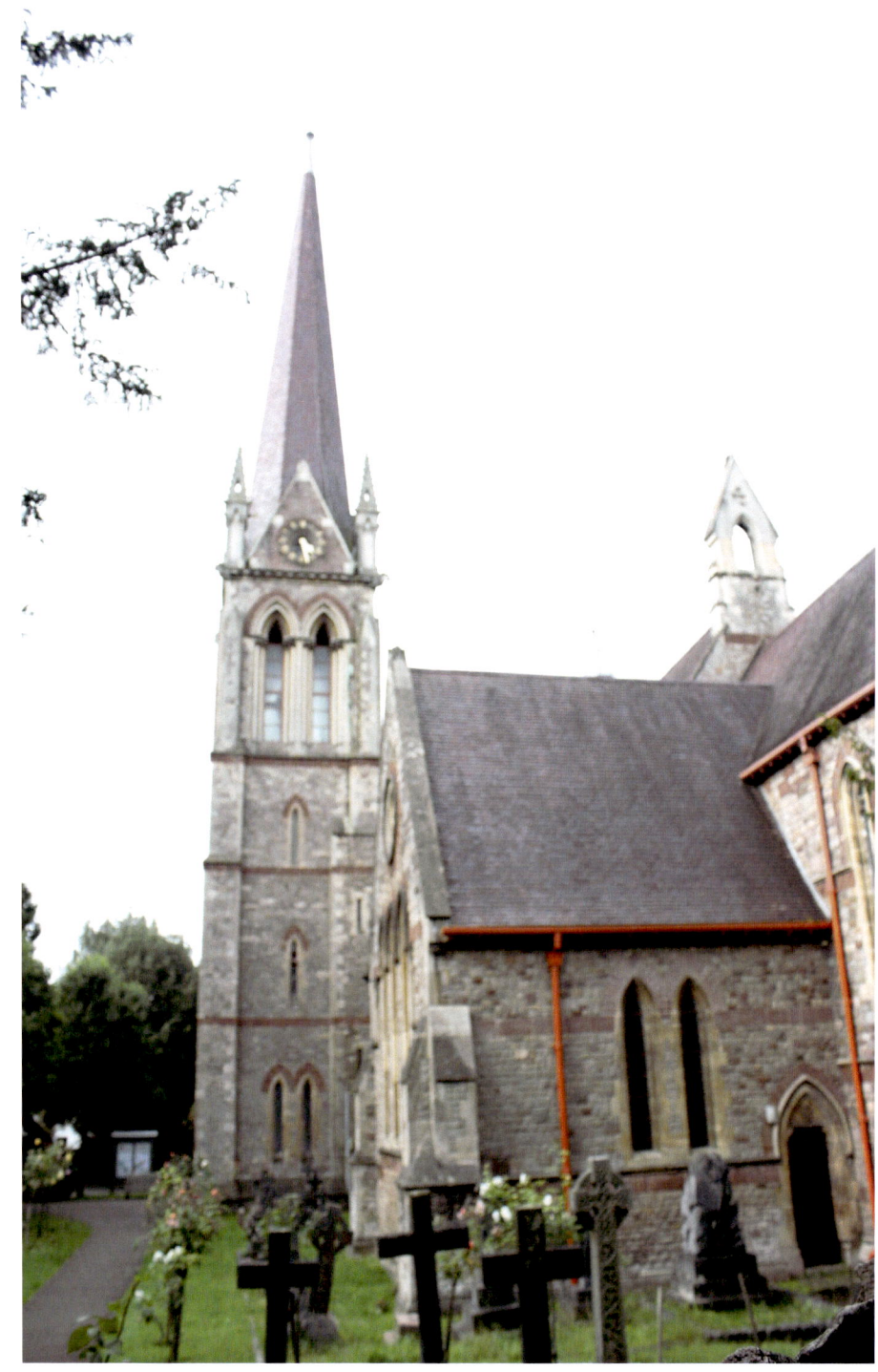

St Mary's Church, Stoke Bishop. (Courtesy of Trevor Naylor)

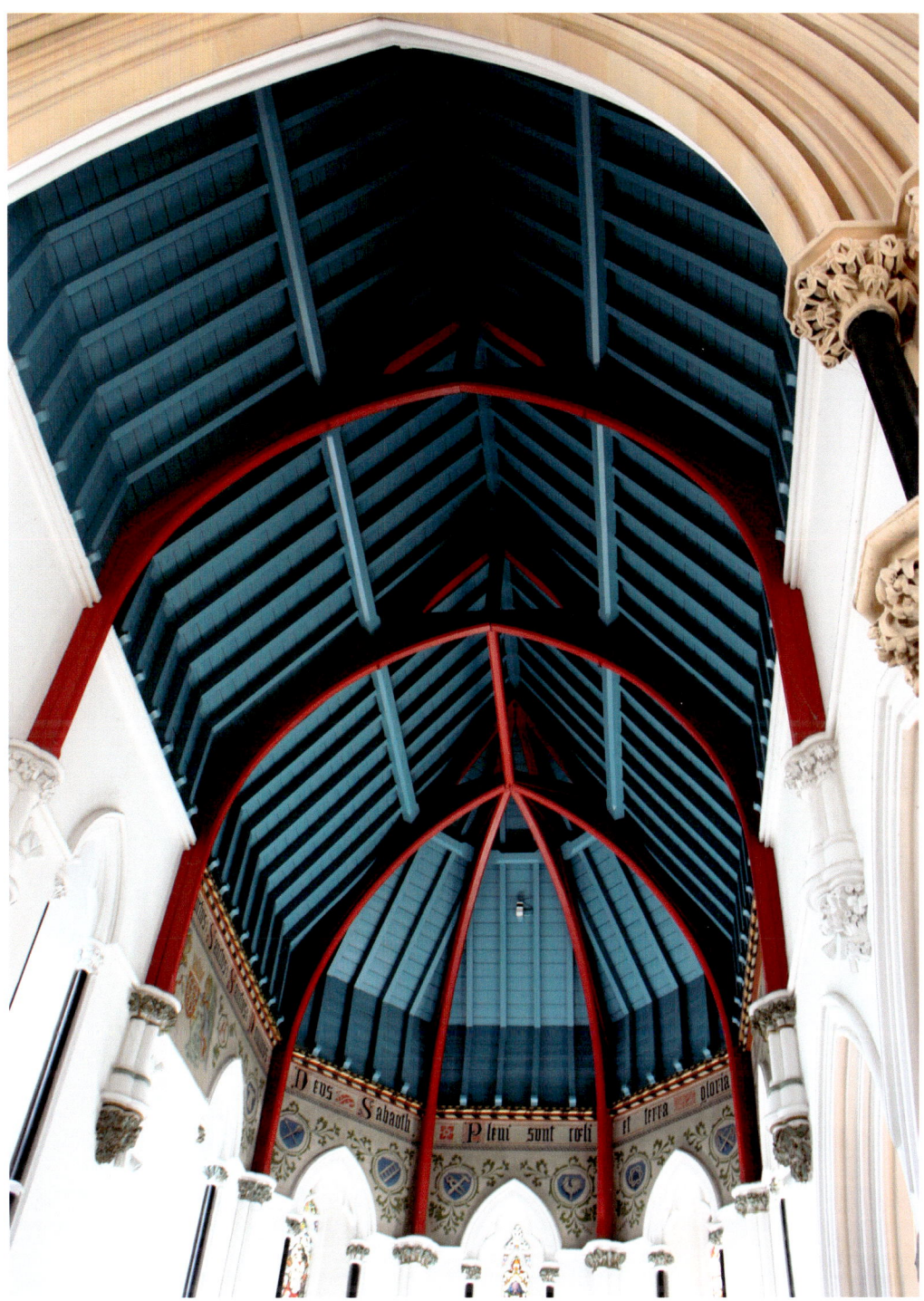

St Mary's Church interior, Stoke Bishop. (Courtesy of Trevor Naylor)

29. Holy Trinity Church, Old Market

Close to the east end of Old Market Street, one of Bristol's widest and busiest commuter thoroughfares, stands the building that was Holy Trinity Church. This was a thriving parish church built by two architects from Birmingham between 1829 and 1832 to support the growing population of Bristol especially in the area east of the original town centre. The church, built with Bath stone, is a Grade II* listed building of Perpendicular Gothic Revival architectural style. Its west front is distinctive because of a pair of octagonal towers of openwork tracery which flank three arched doorways leading into what was the nave. The perimeter walls and railings, which were also designed by the church architects, also have listed building status.

Holy Trinity was part of a programme of church building approved by Parliamentary commissioners. The cost of building it amounted to £8,231, while the land was given to the church authorities by Bristol Corporation. There was a grant from the Parliamentary commissioners of just over £6,000.

Holy Trinity became one of Bristol's most popular parish churches with seating for 2,200 people. The church was packed when it was consecrated by the Bishop of Bristol in 1832. On that occasion 1,500 seats were made available free of charge for those who could not afford to pay the rent for the desirable seats near the front of the nave. The thinking of many churchgoers at the time was that the closer you sat to the altar, the holier you were deemed to be!

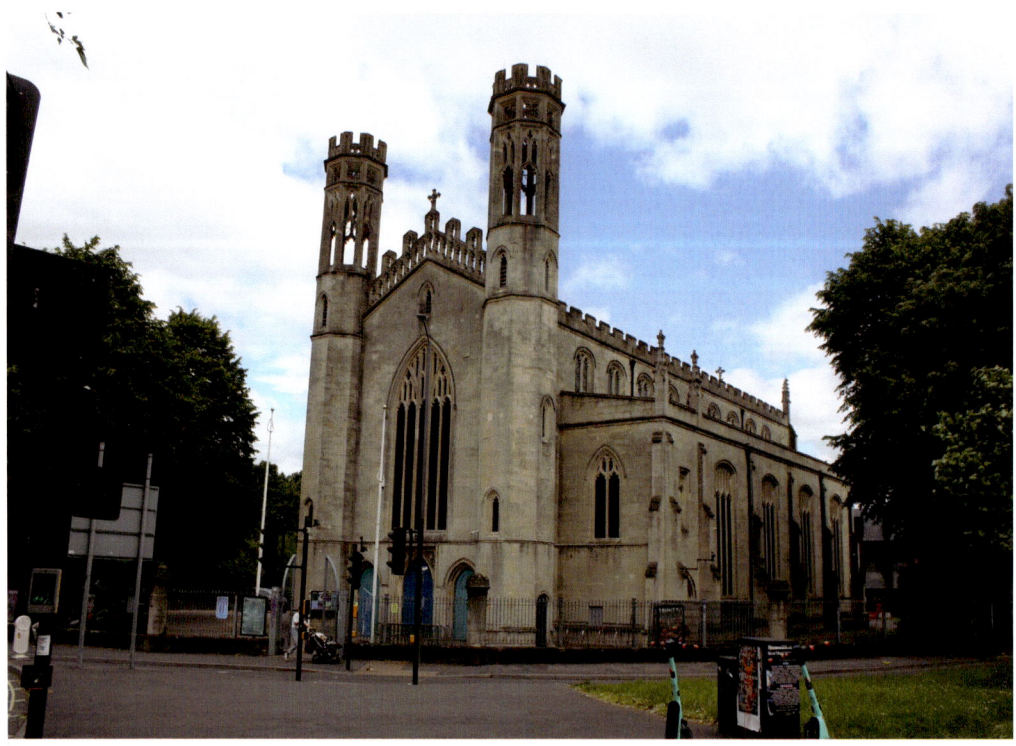

Trinity Church, Old Market, now an arts centre. (Courtesy of Trevor Naylor)

The church was closed in the mid-1970s due to a declining congregation and a lack of funds. The building was deconsecrated and graves in the surrounding churchyard were exhumed. Remains of human beings were reburied at other cemeteries in Bristol. The church is now a music and arts centre called the Trinity Centre. An extra floor has been added near the top of the nave arcade. The building still has the most prominent façade in the Old Market Conservation Area.

Holy Trinity Church is the third place of worship in this particular part of Bristol to have been given a new use. St Paul's Church in Portland Square has become a centre of a contemporary circus while a rock-climbing centre has been built within St Werburgh's Church in Mina Road. The exteriors of all three churches remain been unchanged.

30. St Thomas the Martyr, Redcliffe

Passers-by can be forgiven for missing St Thomas the Martyr Church in the centre of the city, which has often described as a 'Georgian gem'. It stands close to Bristol Bridge and is surrounded by law courts, a music venue and students' residential accommodation, but it is overshadowed by Bristol's first skyscraper office block, built in 1960–63 to a height of 15 storeys. Since then, another floor has been added. At the time protestors said that the office block failed to respond to its environment, in particular its physical relationship to the adjacent church.

The present church of St Thomas is the second by that name to have been built on this same site. The first stood here for 600 years, but towards the end of the eighteenth century the church authorities declared it to be unsafe for use. An Act of Parliament entitled 'An Act for rebuilding the Parish Church and Tower of St Thomas within the city' was passed.

The architect commissioned to design the new church was James Allen, who lived in neighbouring St Thomas Street. He intended to raise and modernise the tower in a classical fashion. For some unknown reason he left the tower untouched but rebuilt the rest of the church. It is described as being of a neoclassical style and was built between 1791 and 1793. Its tower is Perpendicular Gothic. Some of the old church's furnishings were transferred to the new building, including the carved oak altarpiece from the early eighteenth century and a carved pulpit. At the east end of the church is a reredos of 1716 and at the west end a gallery of 1728–32. Nineteenth-century alterations included the reduction of the pulpit and refashioning of the pews. The church, the wall, gates and gateway are all ranked as Grade II* listed buildings.

Many of the people who lived nearby were wealthy weavers and clothiers who generously supported the church.

St Thomas's Church survived the bombs of the Blitz in the Second World War, while many nearby buildings suffered some bomb damage. However, after the war its congregation started dwindling. The last service was held in 1982 and the church was declared redundant. The building has since passed into the care of the Churches Conservation Trust. It is currently leased to a Romanian

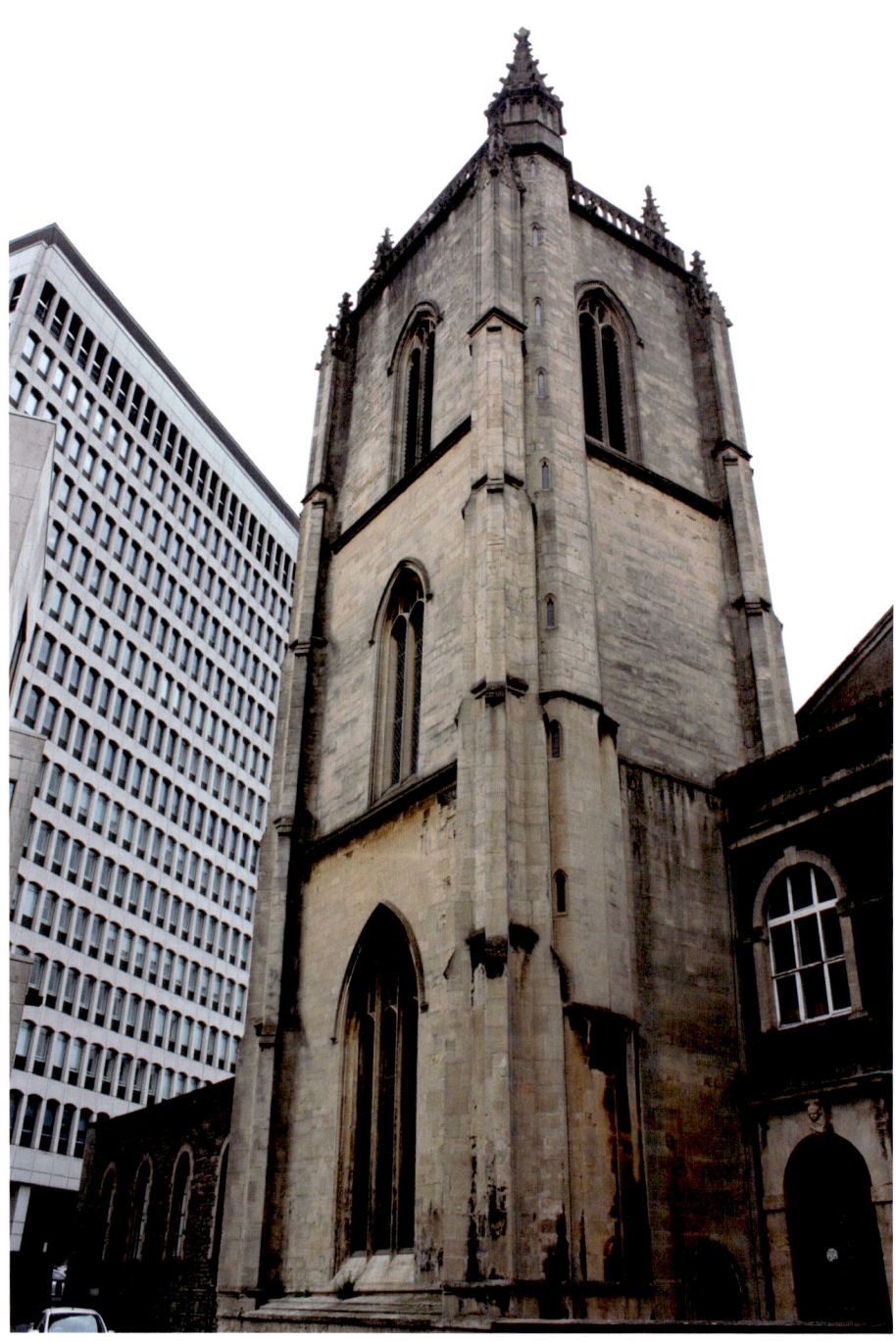

St Thomas, surrounded by commercial buildings. (Courtesy of Trevor Naylor)

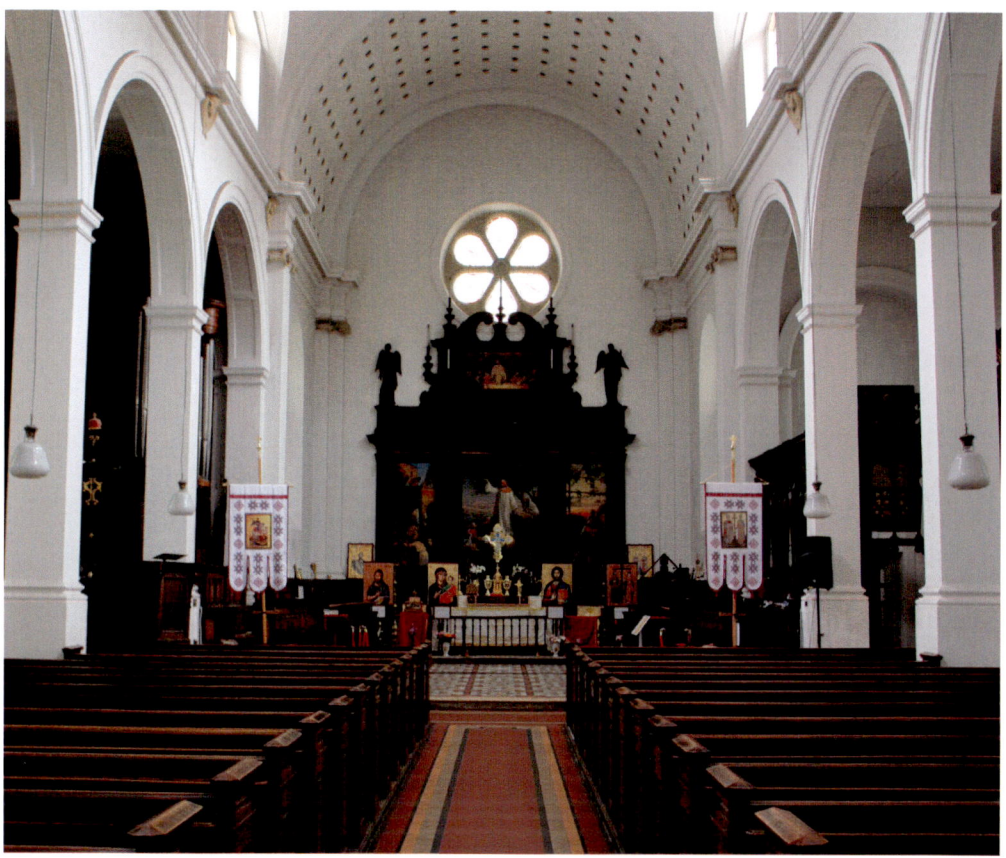

St Thomas, interior view. (Courtesy of Trevor Naylor)

Orthodox church community which uses St Thomas' for worship on Sundays and on special days. The church is also available for hire for performance or exhibition space.

Rather like the original church, the present building is light, airy and spacious. It is said that the first St Thomas Church was second only in elegance to St Mary Redcliffe Church, a walk of less than half a mile away due south.

31. St Mary's Church, Shirehampton

Two years to the day after the first parish church in the suburb of Shirehampton was destroyed by fire a replacement church was officially opened. The fire started in the early hours of Sunday 15 January 1928. Flames quickly burnt almost everything in the church from one end of the building to the other. All furnishings, the organ and stained glass were entirely lost. All that remained was the vestry and the steeple with a bell weighing half a ton. At great personal risk the vicar with the help of the police and people who lived close to St Mary's dragged the safe out of the church along with clergy robes which were taken to a nearby building for safe keeping.

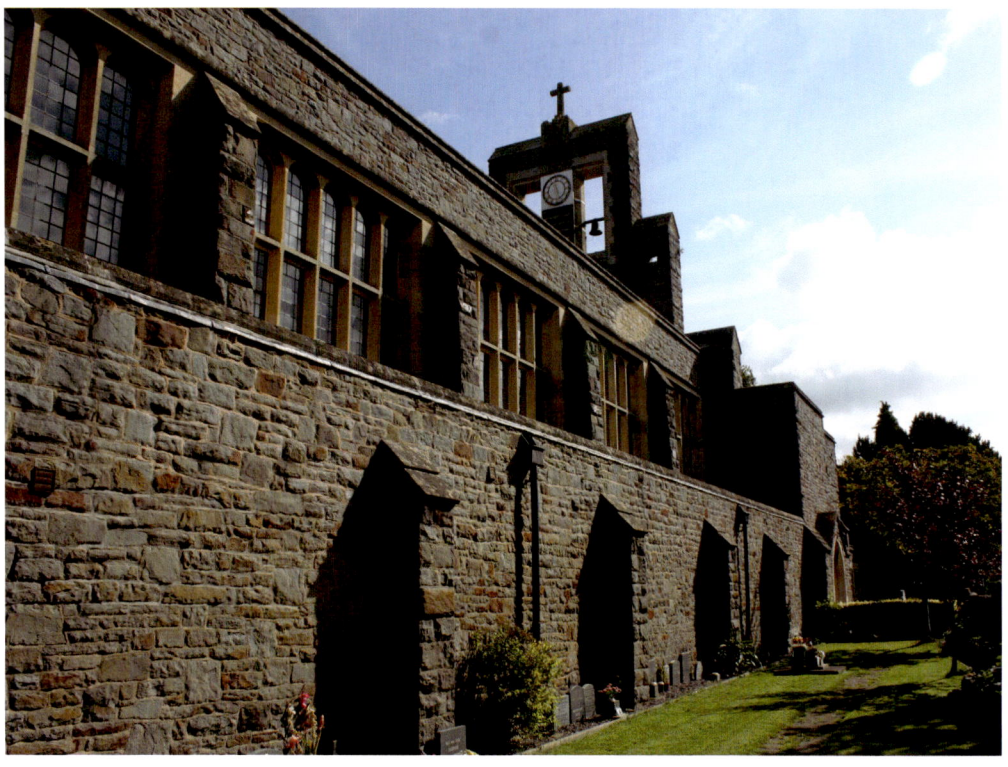

St Mary's Church, Shirehampton. (Courtesy of Trevor Naylor)

The cause of the blaze was never discovered. Church services during the next two years were held at the nearby National School building. Church of England authorities were soon talking about constructing a replacement church. When it was completed there was room for 600 people – double the number as before. The new church was constructed without any wood; it was all reinforced concrete and glass and built in a Gothic Revival style. The cost of the church was £7,000 more than the insurance payout on the old building. The Bishop of Bristol offered half this amount from his appeal fund if the parish would raise the other half.

On 15 January 1930 the new St Mary's Church was consecrated by the Bishop of Malmesbury. The church was packed for this special service with many people having to stand in the churchyard.

St Mary's Church, which is not far from Avonmouth Docks, stands in Shirehampton's vibrant high street alongside shops, pubs and houses on the north-west edge of Bristol.

32. Church of St Mary the Virgin, Henbury

There was probably a church on the site of St Mary the Virgin at Henbury way back in Saxon times. The nave and tower of the present church date from around the twelfth century to the beginning of the thirteenth. It stands upon the site of an old Saxon church.

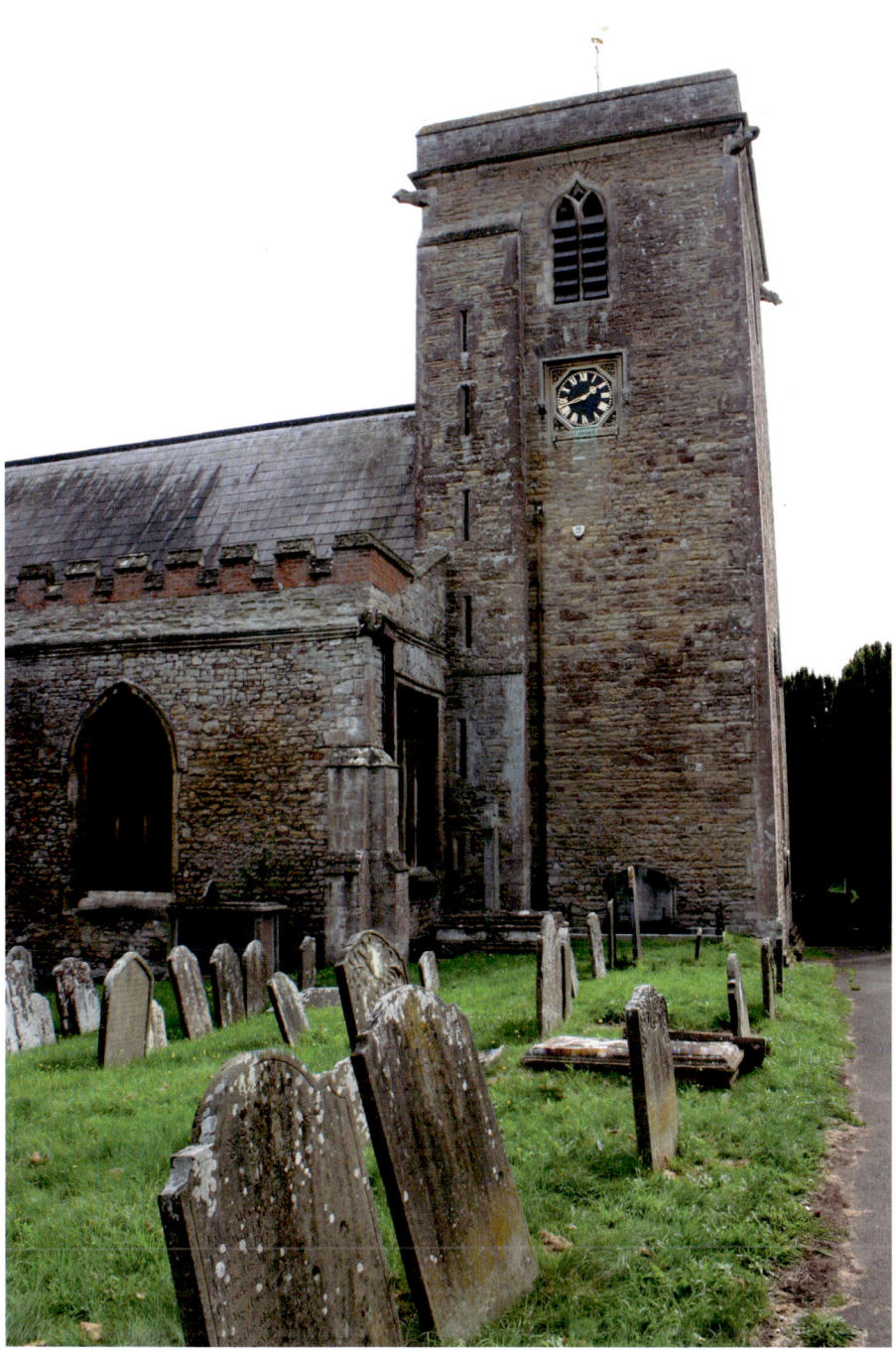

St Mary's Church, Henbury. (Courtesy of Trevor Naylor)

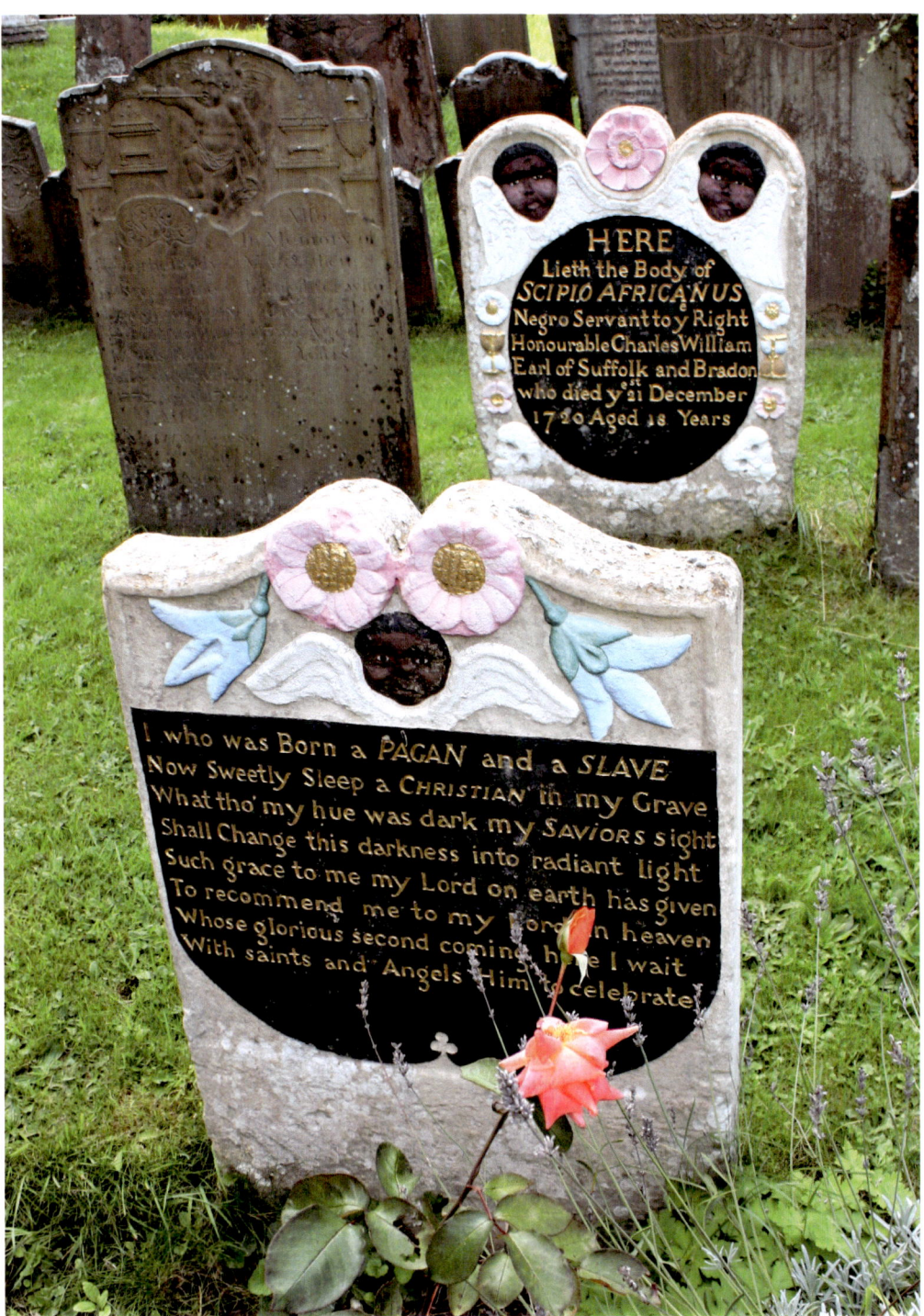

Tombstone of Scipio Africanus at St Mary's Church, Henbury. (Courtesy of Trevor Naylor)

The churchyard of St Mary the Virgin is significant because it contains one of the few graves in this country of a slave. Scipio Africanus was a pageboy dressed in livery working for Charles William, the Earl of Suffolk, who lived in The Great House at Henbury. He must have held Scipio Africanus in high regard for when he died he was buried in a prominent position on the main pathway to the church. He died in December 1720 aged eighteen years.

His gravestone is elaborately painted with the faces of black cherubs. The footstone of the grave is inscribed with a verse which begins with the words: 'I who was Born a Pagan and a Slave now Sweetly Sleep a Christian in my Grave'.

Before being absorbed into Bristol, Henbury was a village in Gloucestershire.

33. St Alban's Church, Westbury Park

Another church building that sprung up because local people wanted a place of worship close to their homes was that of St Alban's in Westbury Park. Back in 1890 some of the 1,200 people living in the area thought that their parish church in Westbury-on-Trym was too far away, especially for those who were elderly or frail and would find it difficult crossing wet fields in winter.

In the summer of 1890 a meeting of residents in Westbury Park discussed the possibility of building a church for their own district. It seems that they

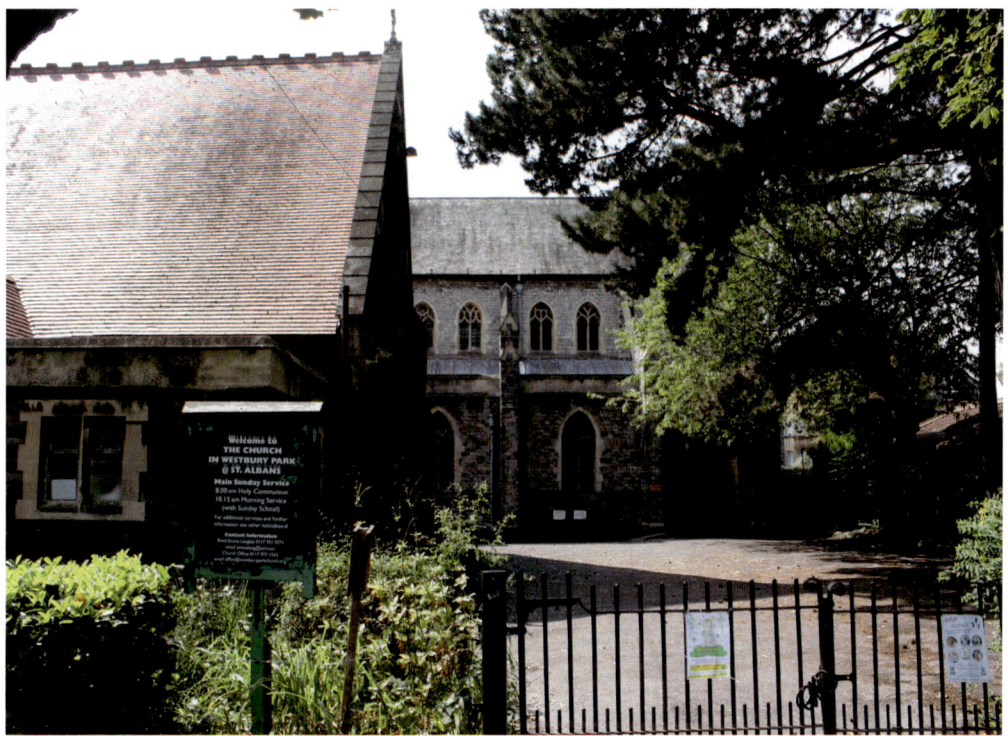

Two churches on the same site at St Albans, Westbury on Trym. (Courtesy of Trevor Naylor)

wasted no time in organising a number of events to raise the necessary money. Early in the New Year a concert was held and six months after that the site for a church was chosen and early in 1892 the foundation stone was laid by the Dean of Bristol. The completed church on Bayswater Avenue was opened in May 1894. A brief entry in *Arrowsmith's Dictionary of Bristol* described the church as being of 'a simple style but well-designed'. It put the cost of the building at around three thousand pounds. However, with more people moving into Westbury Park it turned out that St Alban's church was not big enough to cater for the increasing number of people wanting to go to church.

A competition was held to find the best plan for a much bigger church. It was won by Bristol-based architect C. F. W. Dening, who drew up the most appropriate design. Work started on building the nave, with the Bishop of Bristol laying the foundation stone in November 1907. In the spring of 1909 the Archdeacon of Bristol licensed the new church for public worship. It was reported that a 'vast congregation crowded the aisles and doorways'. A new chancel, clergy and choir vestries and the side chapel were completed for consecration in 1915. Remarkably, the new church was built alongside the old one which has since become the church hall. Besides being used for church social functions the hall has been used by various amateur drama groups to stage their productions. The new church was dedicated by the Bishop of Gloucester and Bristol. St Alban's is the only church in Bristol named after the first English martyr.

34. Redland Church, Redland

When he retired from business in London to live in Bristol, John Cossins not only built a Georgian manor house for himself and his wife, Martha, but also a private chapel nearby.

John Cossins commissioned John Strahan, an architect working in Bristol and Bath, to design his chapel. It was built of Bath stone between 1740 and 1743. A lead cupola surmounted by a ball and cross is a distinctive feature of the building. This Georgian church has been designated by English Heritage as a Grade I listed building. An interior feature of the church is busts of John and Martha Cossins sculpted by Michael Shabrack, the Flemish sculptor who spent most of his career in England.

It is not clear why the chapel was not consecrated until 1790. The chapel has never been dedicated to a patron saint. In 1942 the Church of England created the parish of Redland, thus separating the church that Cossins built from the parish of Westbury-on-Trym.

Little is known about John Cossins, nor the history of his chapel, which is still in use. We do know, though, Cossins was a 'grocer' in London. For more than 130 years his home, Redland Court, was the home of Redland High School for Girls. In 2016 the school merged with Red Maids' School at Westbury-on-Trym. Since then, Redland Court has been converted into private residential accommodation.

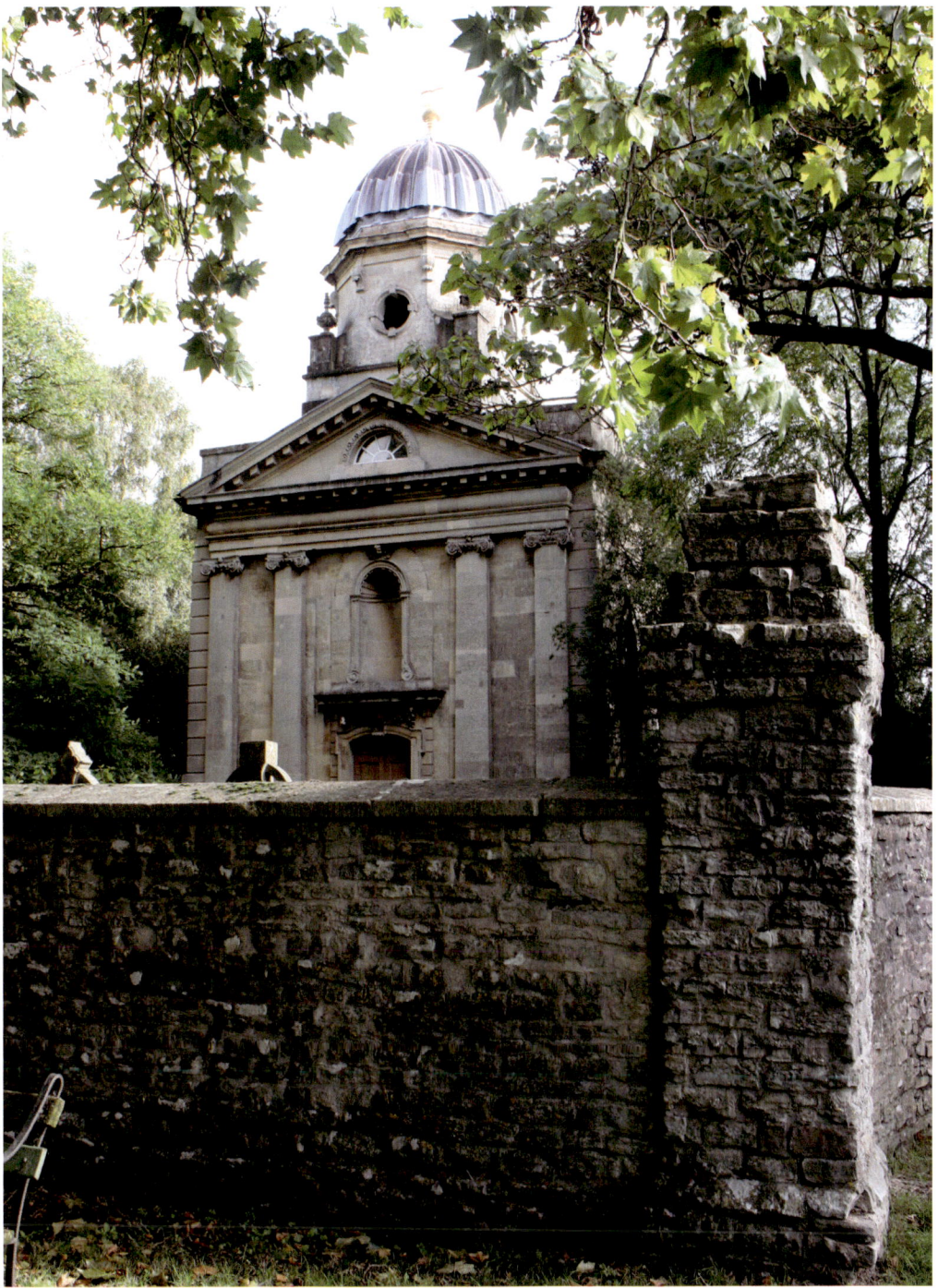

Redland Chapel, exterior view. (Courtesy of Trevor Naylor)

35. The Chapel of the Three Kings of Cologne, Colston Street

At the top of Colston Street, formerly known as Steep Street, just off the city centre, stands what must be the city's smallest place of worship. It is also the only church or chapel in the country dedicated to the Three Kings of Cologne – Caspar, Balthasar and Melchior – also known in the Bible as the Magi (or the Three Wise Men) who visited the infant Jesus with gifts of gold, frankincense and myrrh.

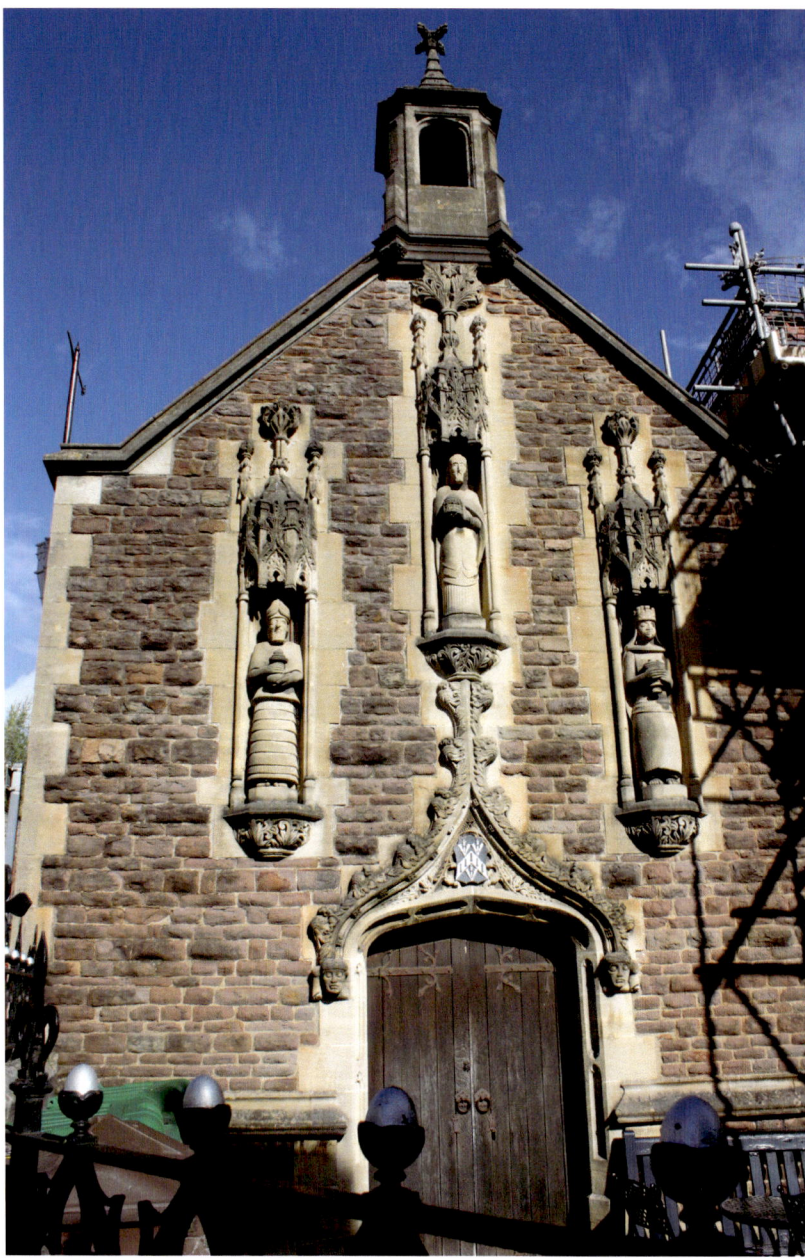

View of the Chapel of the Three Kings of Cologne. (Courtesy of Trevor Naylor)

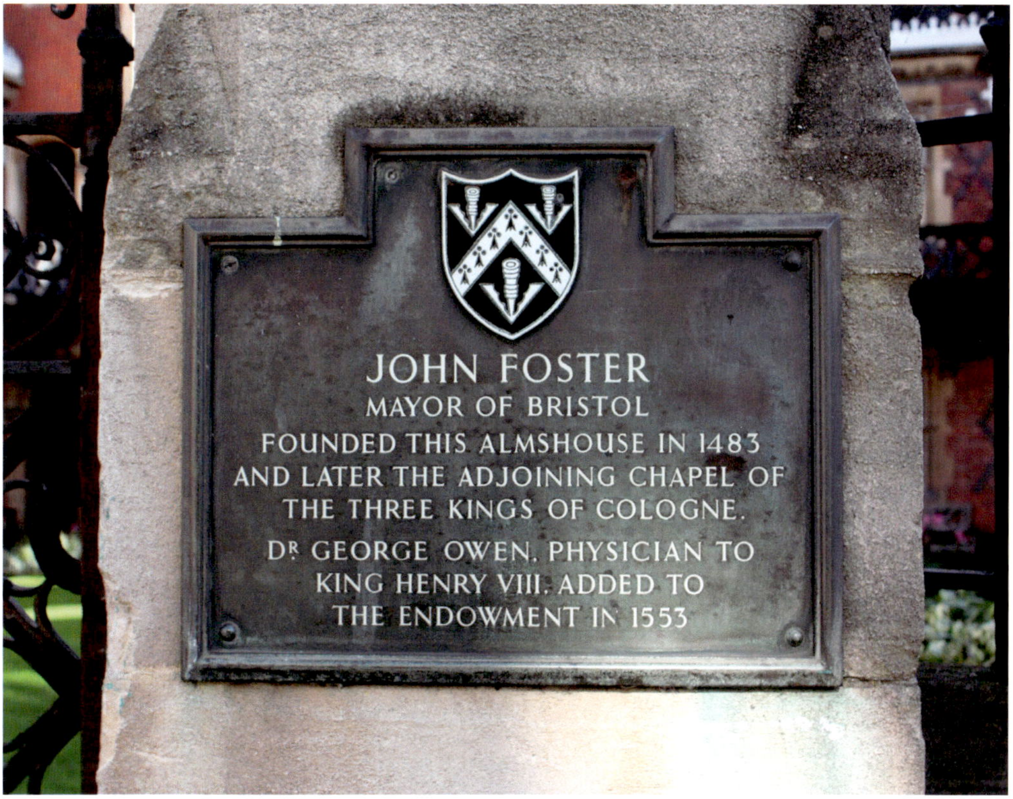

JOHN FOSTER
MAYOR OF BRISTOL
FOUNDED THIS ALMSHOUSE IN 1483
AND LATER THE ADJOINING CHAPEL OF
THE THREE KINGS OF COLOGNE.
Dr GEORGE OWEN, PHYSICIAN TO
KING HENRY VIII, ADDED TO
THE ENDOWMENT IN 1553

Above: Plaque celebrating the founder of the Chapel of the Three Kings of Cologne. (Courtesy of Trevor Naylor)

Right: Stained-glass window in the Chapel of the Three Kings of Cologne. (Courtesy of Trevor Naylor)

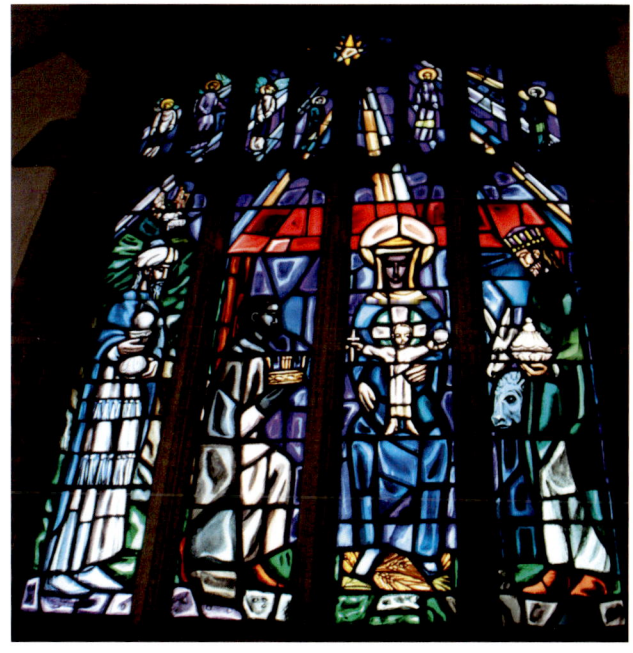

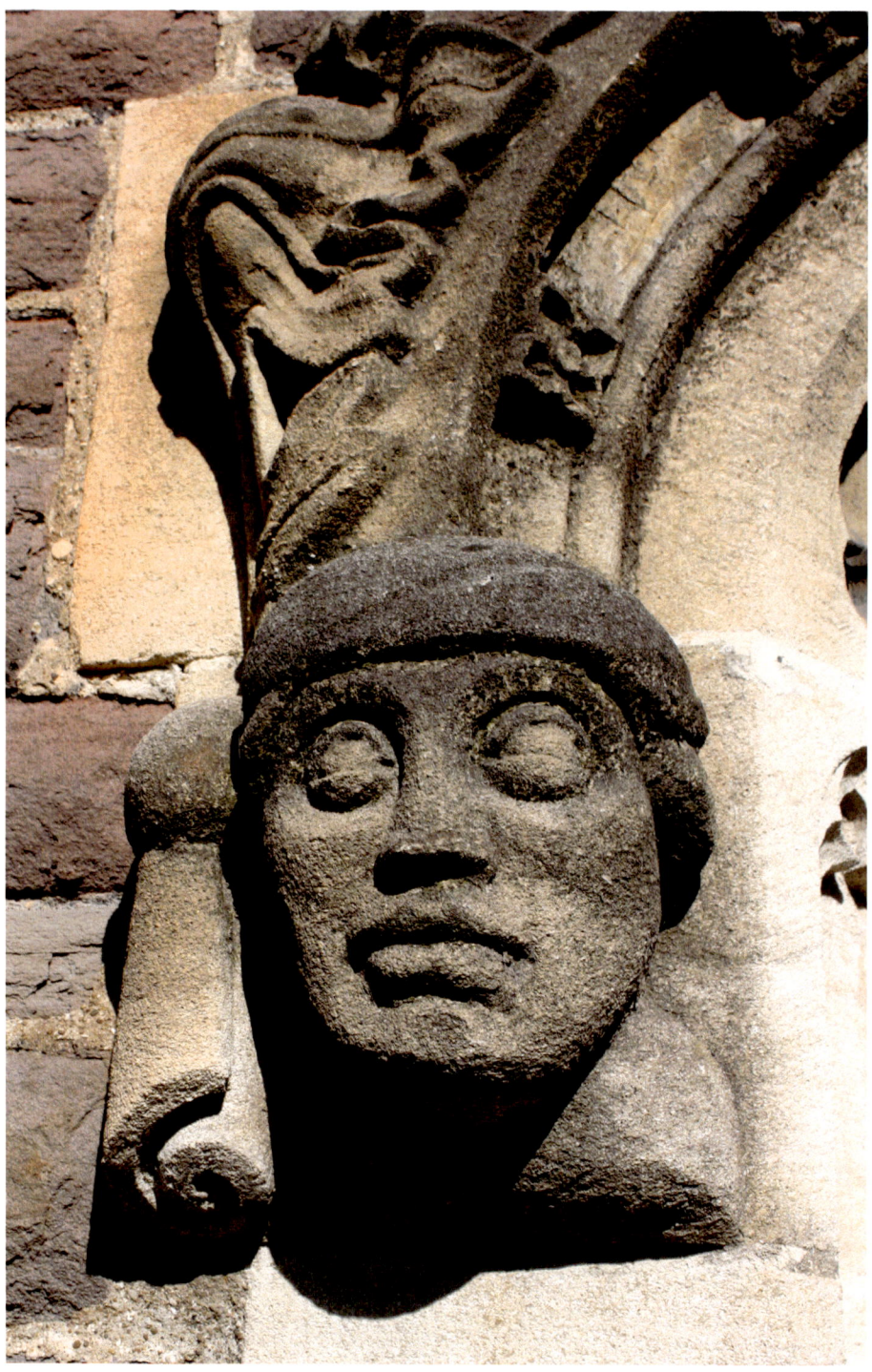

Detail of stonework at the Chapel of the Three Kings of Cologne. (Courtesy of Trevor Naylor)

The Chapel of the Three Kings of Cologne was built in the late fifteenth century along with the adjoining almshouses (now private accommodation) by John Foster, a wealthy salt merchant who lived in the centre of Bristol. At one time he was mayor of Bristol, the city's high sheriff and on another occasion Member of Parliament for the city.

He built the almshouses for thirteen women and an equal number of men. Foster's chapel measures just 18 × 22 feet. It is no surprise then to find that a guided tour on heritage open days is advertised as taking no more than five minutes. The master of the almshouses was responsible for appointing a priest and the maintenance of the chapel.

It is thought that Foster chose the chapel's name after visiting Germany's Cologne Cathedral, where the bones of the Three Kings are said to be kept. It is the only church in England dedicated to the Three Wise Men.

In 2007 the charity that then owned the almshouses and chapel decided they were no longer fit for elderly people and sold them to a property developer so that they could be converted into private accommodation. The residents have use of the chapel as a meeting place.

The chapel backs onto the historic Christmas Steps, which consists of forty-nine steep steps with shops on either side rising from Christmas Street at the bottom to Colston Street at the top. A plaque at the top of the steps tells us that they were 'steppered done and finished' in 1669.

Bibliography

Arrowsmith's *Dictionary of Bristol 1906*

Barnes, Max, *Bristol: A–Z*

Bristol Corporation, *Official Guide to the City of Bristol* (1924)

Henderson, Ray and Keith Sheather, *St Mary Magdalene Church: The Story of Stoke Bishop Church 1860–2000*

Latimer, John, *Annals of Bristol*, Volume I (1900/1908)

Nicholls, J. F. and John Taylor, *Bristol Past and Present*, Volume III (1882)

St Alban's Church, *The First Seventy-five Years*

Thomas, Ethel, *Shirehampton Story*

Underdown, Thomas, *Bristol Under Blitz*

Newspapers and Magazines

Bristol Evening Post – various editions from 1932 onwards

Bristol Evening World – various editions between 1930 and 1960

Various parish magazines from 1900 onwards

Western Daily Press – various editions from 1920 onwards

Acknowledgements

For me, writing books about Bristol is largely a labour of love. I started researching *Churches of Bristol* by delving into my own archives of old newspapers, press releases and other publicity material that I have accumulated working as a journalist on newspapers, radio and television. The *Western Daily Press*, from its first edition in the mid-nineteenth century to the present day, was extremely useful, as was the *Bristol Evening Post* (now the *Bristol Post*) and its weekly local history supplement, *Bristol Times*. Copies of some of Bristol's long-extinct newspapers, especially the *Bristol Evening World*, which ceased publication in the early 1960s, also proved to be a valuable source of information.

Books like these only get written with the help of many other people. I have made many visits to the Reference Section of Bristol Central Library and to Bristol Archives. I am extremely grateful to the staff of both departments who patiently dealt with my numerous enquiries, some of them quite obscure, about Bristol's churches.

About the Author

Bristol born and bred, I have long been passionate about my native city's colourful and rich history. I love delving into archives relating to Bristol's dim and distant past. As a journalist I have held key editorial posts in regional newspapers and radio and television newsrooms. I have written various books about Bristol's history, including *Bristol From the Post and Press,* which was published by Amberley.

I have visited many churches across the city, from St Alban's in Westbury Park to St Thomas in the Redcliffe area (sorry, dear reader, but I couldn't find a church beginning with the last letter of the alphabet). I am also very grateful to the clergy of and staff (many of whom are volunteers) of the churches I visited. They willingly gave me their time as they helped me to search through seldom seen documents and dog-eared parish magazines, some of them dating back more than a hundred years.

Last but certainly not least, I express my sincere and endless thanks to Janet and Trevor Naylor. This is not only for their suggestions about which churches would be interesting to write about but also to Trevor for spending many hours travelling around Bristol to take the photographs, which I believe enhance the quality of this book.